PHP: The Good Parts

Peter B. MacIntyre

O'REILLY®

Beijing · Cambridge · Farnham · Köln · Sebastopol · Taipei · Tokyo

PHP: The Good Parts
by Peter B. MacIntyre

Published by O'Reilly Media, Inc., 1005 Gravenstein Highway North, Sebastopol, CA 95472.

O'Reilly books may be purchased for educational, business, or sales promotional use. Online editions are also available for most titles (*http://my.safaribooksonline.com*). For more information, contact our corporate/institutional sales department: 800-998-9938 or *corporate@oreilly.com*.

Editor: Julie Steele	**Indexer:** Seth Maislin
Production Editor: Adam Zaremba	**Cover Designer:** Karen Montgomery
Copyeditor: Amy Thomson	**Interior Designer:** David Futato
Proofreader: Adam Zaremba	**Illustrator:** Robert Romano

Printing History:

April 2010:	First Edition.

RepKover. This book uses RepKover™, a durable and flexible lay-flat binding.

ISBN: 978-0-596-80437-4

[M]

1270504454

I dedicate this book to my wonderful wife,
Dawn Etta Riley.

I love you!

Table of Contents

Foreword

Why, you might ask, do we need yet another book on PHP? And why, now, is it relevant to point out the "good parts?" Well, this is not just any book, and this is not just any time in the life of PHP. PHP is gaining adoption more rapidly now than ever before, and there are progressively more people who want to know what PHP is and to understand its popularity. With the continuous shift of individuals and enterprises towards deeper adoption of PHP, it is important for the world to have a quick read (and reference) to get the basics of the language before committing to deeper works, larger projects, or training. This is that book. No matter who or what you are today—a nonprogrammer, a Java programmer, or an RPG programmer—there is no better place to quickly start to understand what is good about PHP. Once you have this under your belt, decisions on how to move forward with or without PHP—and whether to delve into it at a deeper level—should become much easier.

I have spent the last three years and more working side-by-side with the team that brought PHP to a place where it could easily be used in business, and I have seen the many ways in which PHP has offered great benefits to enterprises. One example was a single sign-on portal for 1,800 auto dealers and 2,400 service centers (comprising over 42,000 users) to be able to customize, order, and service consumer vehicles in 17 countries across Europe. Integrating 15 disparate software applications to communicate with backend systems is a challenge in any language, but PHP offered a rapid turnaround, quick time-to-market "glue" language solution that enabled this enterprise to accomplish its goals in short order and with cost savings over other possible solutions.

In my former position as the VP of Global Services at Zend Technologies, the progressively increasing demand for PHP within enterprises led us to develop a full portfolio of service offerings, including a strong curriculum of training courses. There was a similar demand from individual developers who benefited from these offerings as well and, despite the recent economic environment (or maybe because of it), we saw no dip in student registration and attendance. I would recommend this book as an excellent precursor to any of those courses.

Peter MacIntyre has, for many years, been instrumental in helping many people gain the benefits of PHP through his writing, teaching, and speaking engagements. I had the pleasure of meeting Peter about three years ago, when I was introduced to him by colleagues at Zend. Peter had completed a couple of webinars for us and my colleagues felt so strongly about his ability to convey valuable information that they believed he would make a great addition to our training team. Since that time, I have continued to watch the many ways in which Peter has spread the word about the ease of using PHP, the many associated technologies and tools available, and the many avenues through which to learn it. He is an ardent user of this technology and knows it and all its associated technologies extremely well.

Peter, in this book, mentions some of the larger visible applications (such as Facebook and Yahoo!), and throughout my involvement with PHP I have seen many large organizations (including JC Penney, Best Buy, DHL, Fox Interactive, GE, and Deutsche-Telecom) use PHP in many ways that show the power of this simple language. Think job opportunities! If you plan to focus on using PHP to develop a career or expand it, you will be interested to know that in conversations with companies like ODesk, I learned that, of all the skills in demand through that site, PHP was one of the top and was at that time generating the highest rate per hour. Rates ran higher for those with a Zend Certified Engineer certification.

I think the most amazing adoption of PHP to date has been that of the IBMi/RPG world. It has been very rewarding to see nonprocedural programmers come into the new age of web development, first with a slight struggle, perhaps, but then with total eagerness once they see what modern interfaces they can provide to their users (or clients), with functionality as sophisticated as PHP can provide on the IBMi. So, if you are an IBMi user or an RPG programmer, buy this book now and you'll soon find yourself under the spell of PHP. Green screens can be modernized and your applications can live on.

What if you are a strong Java programmer and PHP is just, well, "beneath" you? This is always a fun discussion for all us PHP believers! I have heard a number of funny lines: "PHP is not Java" and "Java is dead" and then, from the other side, "PHP is for hobbyists." But all one has to look at is the ramp-up rate of downloads for the Zend Framework, Magento, or Drupal to realize that the simplicity of PHP belies its power and potential. PHP is not a replacement for Java, nor can Java do what PHP can do. These two languages live side-by-side for each of the most successful and leading-edge IT teams. One note of warning, though: read this book carefully—there are different ways to use PHP than a Java programmer would assume based on Java, and this book will guide you on how to leverage PHP for the best results.

Today, over a third of the world's websites are written in PHP, and that number is growing. The language itself has evolved to where it has a complete development infrastructure in place, enabling its sophisticated application to business; Zend Framework, Magento, and Drupal are all very successful examples of this evolution. Market analyst Gartner recently published a report for their clients that forecasted the PHP worldwide developer count to grow to as high as 5 million developers by 2013 (up from 3 million in 2007 and 4 million in 2009). They also provided a short-term forecast indicating that PHP will remain a widely adopted web development technology.

It is time for more people, and for you, to understand what is behind this buzz. So I invite you to go ahead: read on, enjoy, and join the growing family of PHP users! You won't go back.

—Susie Sedlacek
Former VP of Global Services, Zend Technologies

Preface

Conventions Used in This Book

The following typographical conventions are used in this book:

Italic

    Indicates new terms, URLs, email addresses, filenames, and file extensions.

`Constant width`

    Used for program listings, as well as within paragraphs to refer to program elements such as variable or function names, databases, data types, environment variables, statements, and keywords.

`Constant width bold`

    Shows commands or other text that should be typed literally by the user.

`Constant width italic`

    Shows text that should be replaced with user-supplied values or by values determined by context.

 This icon signifies a tip, suggestion, or general note.

 This icon indicates a warning or caution.

Using Code Examples

This book is here to help you get your job done. In general, you may use the code in this book in your programs and documentation. You do not need to contact us for permission unless you're reproducing a significant portion of the code. For example, writing a program that uses several chunks of code from this book does not require permission. Selling or distributing a CD-ROM of examples from O'Reilly books does require permission. Answering a question by citing this book and quoting example code does not require permission. Incorporating a significant amount of example code from this book into your product's documentation does require permission.

We appreciate, but do not require, attribution. An attribution usually includes the title, author, publisher, and ISBN. For example: "*PHP: The Good Parts* by Peter B. MacIntyre. Copyright 2010 Peter B. MacIntyre, 978-0-596-80437-4."

If you feel your use of code examples falls outside fair use or the permission given above, feel free to contact us at *permissions@oreilly.com*.

How to Contact Us

Please address comments and questions concerning this book to the publisher:

> O'Reilly Media, Inc.
> 1005 Gravenstein Highway North
> Sebastopol, CA 95472
> 800-998-9938 (in the United States or Canada)
> 707-829-0515 (international or local)
> 707-829-0104 (fax)

We have a web page for this book, where we list errata, examples, and any additional information. You can access this page at:

> *http://oreilly.com/catalog/9780596804374*

To comment or ask technical questions about this book, send email to:

> *bookquestions@oreilly.com*

For more information about our books, conferences, Resource Centers, and the O'Reilly Network, see our website at:

> *http://www.oreilly.com*

Safari® Books Online

Safari Safari Books Online is an on-demand digital library that lets you easily search over 7,500 technology and creative reference books and videos to find the answers you need quickly.

With a subscription, you can read any page and watch any video from our library online. Read books on your cell phone and mobile devices. Access new titles before they are available for print, and get exclusive access to manuscripts in development and post feedback for the authors. Copy and paste code samples, organize your favorites, download chapters, bookmark key sections, create notes, print out pages, and benefit from tons of other time-saving features.

O'Reilly Media has uploaded this book to the Safari Books Online service. To have full digital access to this book and others on similar topics from O'Reilly and other publishers, sign up for free at *http://my.safaribooksonline.com*.

Acknowledgments

I would first like to thank all those folks at O'Reilly who are involved in books and never really get a pat on the back. I don't even know who you all are, but thanks for all of your work to help get this project done (and done well), and to finally make it to the bookshelves. The editing, graphics work, layout, planning, marketing, and so on all have to be done, and I appreciate your work toward this end.

To Julie Steele, my acquisitions editor at O'Reilly, who always showed great patience and professionalism on this project, thanks for giving me this opportunity and for working with me from start to finish. I think I could now consider you to be one of my better friends in the IT publishing business. One day I hope to meet you in person!

Much thanks to my technical editors, too. Charles Tassell, Brian Danchilla, and Peter Lavin, thanks for your keen eyes and for thoroughly testing my many lines of sample code. Many of your great pointers and ideas were used to make this book better. Wez Furlong and Derick Rethans also contributed some technical pointers; thanks for your assistance as well.

Finally, to Susie Sedlacek, former Vice President, Global Services, Zend Corporation— thanks for being willing to put together an introduction for this book. I was keen to have you do the introduction so that readers could get a global perspective on the ever-growing, worldwide use and impact of PHP. I was happy to hear that you and your husband have purchased a vineyard in California, and I hope that you really enjoy that new endeavor!

CHAPTER 1

The Good Parts

This book has been a rather long time in the making. I have been using PHP for many years now, and have grown to love it more and more for its simplistic approach to programming, its flexibility, and its power. Of all the programming languages I have used throughout my over 20-year career, PHP is my favorite, hands down. PHP has grown from a small set of functions to a very large volume of functions, external interfaces, and add-on tools. Some programmers may be overwhelmed by its apparent vastness, but I hope to show you in this book that most of the PHP world can indeed be of great use. In a relatively short amount of pages, you will be shown all the best areas of the PHP development environment. By the time you get to the last page, you will have a better understanding of how powerful that environment is in the web development sphere.

Why PHP?

With so many programming books on the market these days—and so many PHP books—you might wonder what another book could accomplish. PHP is a widely used language and has experienced much growth in recent years in the enterprise market. Web environments like Facebook, Flickr, portions of Yahoo!, and Wikipedia all use PHP in a significant way, and web content management systems like Drupal, Joomla, and WordPress are also powered by PHP. IBM is also showing a lot of interest in integrating its technologies with PHP. For these reasons, it makes sense for the community to assist beginning and intermediate programmers in becoming familiar with all the best areas of this language.

A Brief History of PHP

Let's start with a brief history of the language. Personal Home Page (PHP), initially known as PHP Tools, was launched in June 1995 by Rasmus Lerdorf. It was originally launched as open source software and remains so to this day. Database integration was implemented in version 2.0 in 1996, and the product has grown by leaps and bounds ever since. Its worldwide use is higher than any other web development language. As of this writing, the latest version of PHP is 5.3, which was released on June 30, 2009.

PHP's Place in the World

PHP is one of the most widely used programming languages in the world. To think that it has grown this much in such a short period of time is quite impressive; in just 15 years or so, it has grown to be one of the major players in the web development world. In the last several years, many members of the PHP community have been debating whether the language is enterprise ready: can it be trusted to handle the big projects and weights? Given the recent focus on PHP from companies like IBM and Microsoft, and the fact that it powers the largest websites in the world (Facebook and Yahoo!), one could argue that it is already in the enterprise. This debate will be resolved over time, but with version 5.3 just recently having been released, it is a safe bet to say that if it isn't, it very soon will be.

What Is PHP?

So what is PHP anyway? It is a scripting language, mostly used on the server side, that can be employed to generate Hypertext Markup Language (HTML) information dynamically. PHP is connected to a web server, generally Apache or Internet Information Server (IIS), and once it has finished generating proper HTML, it sends its creation back to the web server for delivery to the requesting client.

I say "mostly used" on the server side because you can use PHP in many other areas, including command line, desktop PC, and client server environments, just to name a few. However, it is most commonly used in the web server environment.

PHP developers can also integrate PHP with one of many different database tools like MySQL, SQLite, PostgreSQL, DB2, MS SQL, ORACLE, and so on, to make their created content as dynamic as possible. In reality, what is produced is still a static HTML file, but it is produced on the fly and therefore seems to be dynamic. Actually, one could argue that since the content is dynamically drawn out of a database or some other data source, PHP is in fact creating dynamic content.

What Has Been Accomplished with PHP?

Now, saying all these things about PHP and not having any proof would be untoward for sure, so let's take a quick highlight tour of what has been built and accomplished with PHP. Some of the major and most popular web locations in the world are powered at some level by PHP. Table 1-1 includes a short list of popular websites, their Uniform Resource Locators (URLs), and a brief description of what each does.

Table 1-1. Sampling of major websites that use PHP

Website name	Description	URL
Facebook	Social networking	*http://www.facebook.com*
Flickr	Photograph sharing	*http://www.flickr.com*
Wikipedia	Online collaborative encyclopedia	*http://www.wikipedia.org*
SugarCRM	Customer relationship management tool	*http://www.sugarcrm.com*
Dotproject	Project management tool	*http://www.dotproject.org*
Drupal	Website construction template engine	*http://drupal.org*
Interspire	Newsletter and email marketing product	*http://www.interspire.com*

This is only the proverbial tip of the iceberg, and is not in any way meant to be an exhaustive list; it is simply a short list of examples of what has been built with PHP. If you have been to any of these websites, you can see what this powerful language can accomplish.

Basic PHP Setup

By now you might be anxious to try PHP out for yourself, so we'll go through a quick installation discussion here and have you saying, "Hello, world" in no time.

The basic method of PHP development is to build PHP code on top of web server software like Apache or IIS. There is a "stack" of software that is generally used for a fully functional development environment: either LAMP or WAMP. LAMP stands for Linux/Apache/MySQL/PHP, but there are variations to this, as one would expect. You could be using PostgreSQL instead of MySQL for the database and therefore the acronym would be LAPP, but you get the idea. The other acronym—WAMP—stands for Windows/Apache/MySQL/PHP.

> Typically, the OS has no real bearing on the functionality of the written code. PHP written in the Windows environment will certainly operate just as well on a Linux box and vice versa. The only thing to be cautious of is if you are doing OS-level commands like CHMOD (for changing file permissions) or CHOWN (for changing file ownerships) in Linux and want to do the same in a different OS. Just be sure to test your code well in this, and all, instances.

Since there are so many different platforms and components to setting up a full PHP development environment, we won't go into detail on how to establish that environment here. Be sure to go to *http://www.php.net/downloads.php* for a full listing of the latest stable releases for the many and varied platforms. There are also some all-in-one installation packages for Windows; one is called XAMPP (X for cross-platform, A for Apache, M for MySQL, P for PHP, and P for Perl), which can be found at *http://www.apachefriends.org/en/xampp-windows.html*. After you have the package for the appropriate platform, look for a file called *install.txt* among the downloaded files for a setup guide.

Once you have PHP installed, you should be able to run a small script that will interpret your *php.ini* settings file and show you all your directives and setting values. The code for doing this is one line, like so:

```
<?php phpinfo() ; ?>
```

The way to start and stop PHP content is with the `<?php` text sequence and the `?>` text sequence, respectively, but more on that in the next chapter. For now, save this code in your web root folder (usually *www* or *htdocs*) as *phpinfo.php*. When you enter *http://localhost/phpinfo.php* in the browser, the output should resemble Figure 1-1.

Take some time to review these settings, and don't worry if you are not sure what most of them are; simply having a screen that looks like Figure 1-1 is proof enough that PHP is properly installed and being served through your localhost web server.

 Localhost is the web address prefix for all the PHP code you write in your local computer environment. If you have code running off of a remote server, you either reference it with a proper web address or a specific IP number.

Now let's write a little code here to do the proverbial worldwide greeting. Open a file called *HelloOutThere.php* under the document root—typically, this is */var/www/* in Linux or *../apache2/htdocs* in Windows—and enter the following code:

```
<?php  echo "Hello, is there anybody out there?" ; ?>
```

Then enter the following into the browser's address field: *http://localhost/HelloOut There.php*. The result should be a browser page similar to Figure 1-2.

What we are telling the web server to do here is to repeat (echo) something into the browser's display area. With the `echo` command, we can send a string of text or, as you will see later in this book, almost anything within the web context. That's all there is to it. You have just created your first PHP web page.

PHP Version 5.2.10

System	Windows NT PETERMAC-PC 6.0 build 6002
Build Date	Aug 6 2009 12:59:12
Configure Command	cscript /nologo configure.js "--disable-ipv6" "--disable-zts" "--enable-fastcgi" "--disable-bcmath" "--disable-calendar" "--disable-odbc" "--disable-tokenizer" "--disable-json" "--disable-xmlreader" "--disable-xmlwriter" "--without-gd" "--without-sqlite" "--without-wddx" "--enable-cli-win32" "--enable-pdo" "--with-openssl" "--with-libxml" "--with-pdo-sqlite"
Server API	CGI/FastCGI
Virtual Directory Support	disabled
Configuration File (php.ini) Path	C:\Windows
Loaded Configuration File	C:\Program Files\Zend\ZendServer\etc\php.ini
Scan this dir for additional .ini files	(none)
additional .ini files parsed	(none)
PHP API	20041225
PHP Extension	20060613
Zend Extension	220060519
Debug Build	no
Thread Safety	disabled
Zend Memory Manager	enabled
IPv6 Support	disabled
Registered PHP Streams	https, ftps, php, file, data, http, ftp, compress.zlib, compress.bzip2, zip
Registered Stream Socket Transports	tcp, udp, ssl, sslv3, sslv2, tls
Registered Stream Filters	convert.iconv.*, string.rot13, string.toupper, string.tolower, string.strip_tags, convert.*, consumed, zlib.*, bzip2.*

Figure 1-1. Result of phpinfo() function

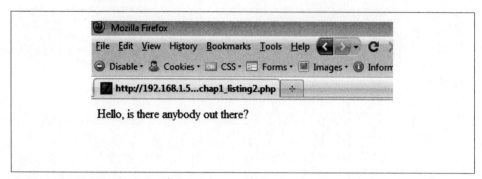

Figure 1-2. HelloOutThere.php example browser output

CHAPTER 2

Casing the Joint

Now that you know the very basics of a PHP file, how to run it through a web server, and how to display some content in a web browser, let's look more closely at the language's building blocks and how you can use them to construct larger, more complex websites and web applications. I call this process *casing the joint* because it involves taking a basic cursory look at the PHP environment to get a better handle on the basics of a PHP code file. The mastery of the building blocks you will be exposed to in this chapter will stand you in good stead, so be sure that you have a strong understanding of them and that you know how and when to use them. Initially, we will look at small segments of a PHP code file (like variables and types of data), and then we will discuss how to control the outcome of a request with the use of decision-making code, also known as *flow control*. Finally, we will explore some concepts that explain the overall environment of a PHP application: where items are placed in memory (server versus client) and how to retrieve information from those areas.

Whitespace, Comments, and Basic Syntax

As far as PHP is concerned, whitespace is ignored when code is sent to the interpreter. This means that all comments and blank lines are effectively stripped out of the code file as it is running.

 If you're trying to achieve microoptimization and want to send some really clean code to the interpreter so that it doesn't have to take time to strip out all the whitespace, look into the PHP function called `php_strip_whitespace`. This function will scan over a code file when provided with the filename, and will clean out all the comments and blank lines, returning the cleaned-out file to you for saving.

If you look at the following code example, you will see many whitespace specimens:

```
1 <?php
2 # this is a PHP comment line
3
4 /*
5 * this is a multi-line PHP
6 * comment block
7 */
8
9 echo "Hello my good web browser" ;    // an inline code comment
10
11
12
13   ?>
```

Line 1 may or may not have some whitespace in it. If you add spaces (by pressing the spacebar) after the opening PHP tag, that would be considered whitespace.

All of line 2 is considered whitespace because it is a *comment line*. Comment lines are notes about the code that are not executed by the PHP interpreter. Lines 4 to 7 are comments as well, but are of a different type. They are known as multiline comment blocks and, as you can see, they begin with a /* combination and terminate with the reverse */ combination. The PHP interpreter considers these four lines as nonexecutable code, and essentially treats it as whitespace, skipping it entirely.

Line 9 is executable, yet it also has an inline comment, signified by the // combination. PHP interprets the comment section first, ignoring it. In fact, the comment can even come between the end of the code and the placement of the semicolon, but that could add confusion to the readability of your code (you will become great friends with the semicolon character as you become more experienced with PHP, because it marks the end of all PHP commands—you will get a syntax error if any are missing).

Lines 3, 8, and 10–12 are empty lines within the file and therefore are neither comments nor executable code. Consequently, they are also considered whitespace. If we removed all the whitespace from this sample it would look like the following:

```
1 <?php echo "Hello my good web browser" ; ?>
```

As you can see, there is some need for small amounts of whitespace between the different commands so that PHP can make necessary distinctions. Also, it is good to note that comments certainly have their place in making the code more human-readable. After all, humans have to read and understand your code in order to maintain it. You can create a comment within a PHP code file using any of the following:

#

> Use this method to indicate an inline comment. You cannot include any executable code on the same line.

//

> Use this method to indicate an inline comment. This can appear on its own line of code or added at the end of an executable line.

`/* ... */`

This indicates a multiline comment block. Do not place any executable code within this block of text.

So, the basic syntax of a PHP statement includes an opening PHP designation tag [`<?php` or `<?`] and a closing tag [`?>`]. These tags allow the web server to determine which portions of the file should be handed over to PHP.

 Use of the shorter open tag format `<?` has depreciated and only works in PHP 5 if the `short_open_tag` directive is enabled. It is much better practice to use the full open tag `<?php` wherever possible.

After this combination of tags, you can begin adding PHP programming statements. You can use one of four different language constructs: statements like the `echo` command, function calls (either from a PHP library or one of your own), flow control statements (`if... else...`), or comments. PHP applications are built on these four simple constructs and, naturally, an entire web application will make use of all of them in large quantities. Additionally, you can define object-oriented classes in PHP (see Chapter 6).

You can also use other combinations of the building blocks of PHP, like variables, to make the application much more robust. Let's take a look at variables and how you can use them.

Variables: Data Types, Loose Typing, and Scope

Variables can hold different kinds of data, but they are always established the same way. Use the following rules when defining a PHP variable:

`$`
Variable names have to begin with a dollar sign (`$`).

Case-sensitive
The name of a variable is case-sensitive, so `$firstname` is a completely different variable than `$FirstName`.

Letter or underscore
After the dollar sign, the next character in the name must be a letter or an underscore; after this, the remainder of the variable name can be any combination of letters, numbers, and underscores.

`$this`
The variable named `$this` is reserved for use in Object Oriented PHP, so it can't be used elsewhere.

A *data type* is simply that: a type of data. These types come with various restrictions on the structure, interpretation, or operations that may be performed on the data. In

PHP, there are eight basic (or *primitive*) variable types; other types may be defined, but we will only be looking at these eight within the scope of this book. The primitive types are categorized in segments: *scalar*, *compound*, and *special*. Table 2-1 shows these types and segments, and gives some examples.

Table 2-1. PHP data types

Segment	Type	Description/example
Scalar types	Boolean	Logical TRUE or FALSE
	Integer	Whole numbers: e.g., 1, 15, −122, and 967967
	Float (double)	Numbers with decimal notations (usually seen in financial situations): e.g., 12.56 or 345.456
	String	Characters, letters, or numbers (usually defined within double quotes): e.g., "Hello there" or "123AvR"
Compound types	Array	A collection of keys with their values, arrays can hold other arrays (multidimensional); see Chapter 5 for more detail
	Object	The basics for class definitions and object-oriented programming; see Chapter 6 for more detail
Special types	NULL	Defines a variable with no value; the variable exists, but contains nothing (not an empty string, not the value 0, nothing)
	Resource	Stores a reference to functions, databases, files, or other resources outside of PHP

There are two ways to assign values to variables: *by value* and *by reference*. The typical way to do assignments is to define by value. For example, in `$firstname = "Peter"`, we are assigning the entire string of five characters to the variable called `$firstname`, and that value will remain intact until it is reassigned or the script has completed. Nothing else can affect that variable content unless the program directly interacts with it.

The reference approach allows the same variable content to use different names, and allows a function to affect a variable that is not part of that function. Only variables previously defined by value can be defined by reference. However, once a variable is assigned by reference, it is tied to its referenced variable; if the content of one of the referenced variables changes, all the local copies of that referenced variable are automatically updated with the new content. To define a variable by reference, simply prefix the referenced variable with the ampersand (&) character. The following code sample shows this in effect:

```php
<?php
    $firstname = "Peter" ;        // assigned by value
    $fname = &$firstname ;
    // $firstname is assigned to $fname by reference.
    echo $fname . "<br/>";        // Peter is displayed
    $fname = "Dawn";              // change referenced value
    echo $firstname  . "<br/>";   // Dawn is displayed, not Peter,
                                  // because of the "by reference"
?>
```

Unlike some other programming languages, PHP is *loosely* or *dynamically typed*. That means that PHP is smart enough to recognize the type of data being stored into a variable at the same time it is being assigned, be that a date, a string, a number, etc. So for the assignment of $firstname = "Peter" in the previous example, PHP can determine that the variable $firstname has a string data type. It is, however, a good practice to predefine the type of data that each variable will be storing, to cut down on confusion.

The *scope* of a variable pertains to what segments of code can see and manipulate the variable in question. By default, variables are within the scope of an entire PHP code file (file-wide scope), but there are exceptions. If a function is defined or included within a code file, variables defined within that function cannot be accessed in other parts of the code file. Another code sample will make this clear:

```php
<?php
    function show_stuff() {
        $secondName = "Beck" ;
        echo "inside show_stuff: " . $firstname . " " . $secondName ;
    }

    $firstname = "Peter" ;        // variable has file-wide scope
                                  // (excluding functions)
    echo $firstname  . "<br/>";   // Peter is displayed
    show_stuff () ;               // only Beck is displayed because $firstname is
                                  // not within the scope of the function,
    echo "Outside function " . $secondName ;
                                  // only defined within the show_stuff function,
                                  // so the overall file cannot access it, and
                                  // nothing will be displayed
?>
```

As you can see, the scopes of the two variables are not the same. $firstname cannot be accessed within the show_stuff function and $secondName cannot be referenced outside the function in which it is defined. There will be more on functions and how you can adjust this default behavior in Chapter 3. For now, recognize that there are areas within code that can be naturally accessed by variables, and other areas that cannot, due to scope.

Defined Constants

A cousin to the PHP variable is the *defined constant*. This is an entity that you can define anywhere in the code file, generally close to the beginning of the code or in a function. A defined constant holds its value until the script has completed. The scope of a defined constant is global, meaning it is file-wide *and* within any defined function or class that is also part of that code file, including any other included files or functions. The rules for defining a constant are similar to those that govern variables, but not exactly the same. The major difference is the use of the built-in PHP function define(). When defining a constant, you must adhere to the following rules:

define()
> Use this PHP function to define the constant.

Letters and underscores
> A constant must start with either a letter or an underscore character, followed by letters, numbers, or underscores.

Case-sensitive
> By default and convention, a defined constant is uppercase, although you can alter this within the `define()` function's options.

Restrictions
> Only scalar data (see the section "Variables: Data Types, Loose Typing, and Scope" on page 9) can be stored in a constant.

So the syntax for defining a constant is as follows:

```
define("name of constant", value of constant, [case insensitive])
```

The case-sensitive parameter at the end of the definition is optional, and by default is false, meaning that the defined constant is in fact case-sensitive (this is considered standard practice). To access the values within a defined constant, make reference to its name. The following code example creates two constants and attempts to recreate one of them.

```
define("SYS_OWNER", "Peter");
define("SYS_MGR", "Simon", true);
echo "System owner is:" . SYS_OWNER . "<br/>" ;
define("SYS_OWNER", "Michael");
echo "System owner is:" . SYS_OWNER . "<br/>" ;
echo "System manager is:" . SYS_MGR . "<br/>" ;
echo "System manager is:" . SYS_mgr . "<br/>" ;
```

The output of this code (with the returned error) is shown in Figure 2-1.

Figure 2-1. Output for defined constant sample code

If PHP error reporting is disabled, you will not get the warning shown in Figure 2-1 and you may have unexpected or unwanted results, so be sure to test your code well before sending it to a production environment.

Defined constants definitely have their place in the PHP world; their worth becomes apparent when you have values that should not change throughout a code script, like a path variable where PDFs are stored, or a tax rate. Be sure to use this feature as much as you need, but also be sure that you test well before sending anything into the production world so that you are getting the results you expect from your constants.

Expressions

Expressions in PHP (not regular expressions; they are a special case) are merely a collective term for code statements.

```
$name = "Peter" ;
```

That single code line is an assignment expression. It states, "assign the string value of *Peter* to the variable called $name." Technically, the code line is a statement (the semicolon is the end-of-statement delimiter) composed of two expressions: the left side is an expression defining the storage and the right side is an expression defining the value to be assigned to the storage. The two expressions together form an assignment expression, and this is the complete statement.

 As a general rule, any assignment of a value is considered an expression, while statements are instructions.

Other types of expressions include some functions and ternary **if** statements (explained in the next section on decision-making code). Functions that return a value are included, for instance. Here are two expression examples:

```
function MyName () {
    Return "Peter" ;
}
$name = MyName();
$name ? $last = "MacIntyre" : $last = "" ;
```

Function MyName is considered an expression since it returns a value, and the weird line of code after that assigns a value to $last based on the condition of the $name variable. We will look at more expressions throughout the book, but for now just be aware that expressions exist and that they are very common within PHP.

Decisions, Decisions (Flow Control)

Code would be quite boring if there were always only one way through it, with no alternate courses and no varying outcomes. The next area of PHP that we will look at is the decision processes that you can define using flow control statements. Flow control statements are used to make decisions based on preprovided conditions.

If...Else...

The basic `if` statement can assign a value or perform other tasks based on the outcome of a simple (or sometimes complex) test. The following code sample uses the `if` statement:

```
$today = date("l") ;
if ($today == "Wednesday") $tax_rate = $tax_rate + 4 ;
```

Notice here that the condition being tested (whether it is Wednesday) is tested with double equals signs. Assignments are made with a single equals sign and tests of equality are done with two of them.

If you want to test for equality at the data type level, you can use the = = = test, which evaluates both the content of the elements being tested and the data types of those items. Consider this code:

```
if (1 == '1') echo "true 1 equals '1' <br/>";
if (1 === '1') echo "true 1 equals '1'";
    else echo "false 1 does not equal '1' " ;
```

This produces the following output, showing that when a string value is compared with a numerical value with = =, the string is converted to a number before the evaluation is performed, thus producing a true result. When comparison is performed with = = = (triple equal), no numerical conversion is done and the evaluation is performed based on both content and data type. Here is the output:

```
true 1 equals '1'
false 1 does not equal '1'
```

There are a number of valid formats you can use when coding an `if` statement. The one above merely performs an equality test and, if it proves to be true, increases the tax rate variable by 4. If the day of the week is anything other than Wednesday, the tax rate remains unchanged. If there are other statements you want to call based on a true condition of the equality test, you can enclose that code with curly braces {like so}. Following is some code that expands on the previous example, while trimming down the test to a direct testing of the returned date value.

```
if (date("l") == "Wednesday") {
    $tax_rate = $tax_rate + 4 ;
    $wages = $salary * 0.4 ;
    $msg_color = "red" ;
}
```

This example executes three statements when the condition test resolves to true. Notice that these three statements are enclosed within opening and closing curly braces to signify that they are all part of that single equality test.

You can also expand the `if` statement to execute code when the false portion of the condition is met; this is called the `else` clause, and this is what it looks like:

```
if (date("l") == "Wednesday") {
    $tax_rate = $tax_rate + 4 ;
    $wages = $salary * 0.4 ;
    $msg_color = "red" ;
} else {
    $tax_rate = $tax_rate + 2 ;
    $wages = $salary * 1.4 ;
    $msg_color = "blue" ;
}
```

The code within the curly braces following the `else` statement will only be executed if the condition resolves to false—in this case, it will execute if the day of the week is any day other than Wednesday.

You can even *nest* the `if` statements within one another. For example, if today was in fact Wednesday and it was the month of June, you could write code that would test for that, like this:

```
if (date("l") == "Wednesday") {
    $tax_rate = $tax_rate + 4 ;
    $wages = $salary * 0.4 ;
    $msg_color = "red" ;
    if (date("F") == "June") {
        $discount = $tax_rate * 0.15 ;
    }
}
```

 Nesting can become cumbersome, so be careful how many levels deep you go because you may end up with unreadable and unworkable code.

You can also write the `if` statement with an `elseif` clause that can perform multiple condition testing as if you were going down a set of steps. So, for example, if you were doing further testing based on the day of the week, you could have code similar to the following example, performing different programming tasks for each day.

```
$weekday = date("l") ;

$tax_rate = 4 ;

if ($weekday == "Monday") {
    $discount = $tax_rate * 0.05 ;
} elseif ($weekday == "Tuesday") {
    $discount = $tax_rate * 0.06 ;
} elseif ($weekday == "Wednesday") {
    $discount = $tax_rate * 0.07 ;
} elseif ($weekday == "Thursday") {
    $discount = $tax_rate * 0.08 ;
} elseif ($weekday == "Friday") {
    $discount = $tax_rate * 0.09 ;
} elseif ($weekday == "Saturday" || $weekday == "Sunday") {
    $discount = $tax_rate * 0.10 ;
```

```
    }
    echo $weekday . "'s discount is: " . $discount ;
```

If you ran this code on a Thursday, the output would look like this:

Thursday's discount is: 0.32

Also note the use of the OR (| |) condition test for Saturday and Sunday.

Another way to write an if statement is to use a *ternary statement*. The format of this statement is not as clear-cut as the if/else statements, but once you master it you can have very succinct code. Let's break the if statement that we just used into this syntax format using only the piece that affects the tax rate. Consider this code:

```
    $tax_rate += date('l') == 'Wednesday' ? 4 : 2;
```

This code is really saying, "If the day of the week is Wednesday, (?) increase the tax rate by 4, otherwise (else, :), only increase it by 2."

 You are probably wondering what is going on with the += notations in this example. PHP allows for a short form of assigning values and doing some math at the same time. ++, --, +=, and so forth are all in this category; be sure to look these up on php.net (*http://php.net/index.php*) to make good use of them.

Ternary tests like this are usually limited to one resulting statement for each potential result (true or false) because if you try to nest them, they may work but may not return the results you are expecting. It's better to keep this kind of code as straightforward as possible.

We are not going to explore every nuance of the if statement here, as there are number of different ways in which to write them and they all work very well. Be sure to look into the other formats on php.net (*http://php.net/index.php*) if you are interested.

Switch...Case...

The if statement can be really limiting (or frustrating) when you want to perform multiple tests on a single value. In our example with the day-of-the-week test, we can actually do seven different things in our code if we so desire. Up to this point, our code only defines a special case if the day happens to be Wednesday. However, if we want a different tax rate for each day of the week, we write our code like this:

```
    $today = date("l") ;
    if ($today == "Monday")    { $tax_rate += 2 ; }
    if ($today == "Tuesday")   { $tax_rate += 3 ; }
    if ($today == "Wednesday") { $tax_rate += 4; }
    if ($today == "Thursday")  { $tax_rate += 5 ; }
    if ($today == "Friday")    { $tax_rate += 6 ; }
```

```
if ($today == "Saturday")    { $tax_rate += 7 ; }
if ($today == "Sunday")      { $tax_rate += 8; }
```

And if we want to do more unique things for each day of the week, the code will be that much more complex and difficult to manage. Enter the **switch...case...** statement. You can use this decision-making construct in situations where there are many possible values. The syntax is as follows:

```
switch (value being tested) {
    case first possible value:
        // run some code
        [break;]
    case 2nd possible value:
        // run some code
        [break;]
    default:
        // if nothing else is true, do this
}
```

This syntax looks a little convoluted, but once you understand its logic it really does make sense. The value within the brackets is the item being tested, followed by each value for the case that you want to evaluate. Finally, if there are other possible values, encase them within the default section.

The break statements are optional, but if you don't use them, PHP will continue to evaluate all the other possible values and may execute some code further down the case tree, so be careful to use the break statements where they make sense.

Our day-of-the-week example, then, would look like this:

```
switch ($today) {
    case "Monday" :
        $tax_rate += 2 ;
        $wages = $salary * 0.2 ;
        $msg_color = "red" ;
        break;
    case "Tuesday" :
        $tax_rate += 3 ;
        $wages = $salary * 0.3 ;
        $msg_color = "yellow" ;
        break;
    case "Wednesday" :
        $tax_rate += 4 ;
        $wages = $salary * 0.4 ;
        $msg_color = "black" ;
        break;
    case "Thursday" :
        $tax_rate += 5 ;
        $wages = $salary * 0.5 ;
        $msg_color = "green" ;
        break;
```

```
    case "Friday" :
        $tax_rate += 6 ;
        $wages = $salary * 0.6 ;
        $msg_color = "orange" ;
        break;
    case "Saturday" :
    case "Sunday" :
        $tax_rate += 7 ;
        $wages = $salary * 0.7 ;
        $msg_color = "purple" ;
        break;
}
```

There is no need here for a default clause, as we are testing for all possible values. But do note that the **break** has been eliminated between Saturday and Sunday, setting the same tax rate for the whole weekend. This is one example of when it might be useful to exclude the **break** statement.

As you can see, the **switch...case...** construct has its advantages. It may still be just as long in terms of lines of code, but the structure of it makes it easier to read and edit.

While...

Now let's talk about the **while** statement. This statement will run code repeatedly as long as a condition remains true. The syntax for this takes two basic forms. First is the straight **while** statement, which looks like this:

```
$repeat = 1 ;
while ($repeat <= 25) {
    echo "the counter is: " . $repeat . "<br/>" ;
    $repeat ++ ;
}
```

The second syntax style (**do...while...**) looks like this:

```
$repeat = 0 ;
do {
    $repeat ++ ;
        echo "the counter is: " . $repeat . "<br/>" ;
} while ($repeat <= 25);
```

The major difference between these two styles is that the **do...while...** construct will execute the code at least once, then validate its test to see if it should be repeated or not. The first sample has the potential to never execute its conditional code. If, for example, $repeat is set to 27 rather than 1 in the first line, the test will resolve to false and the code inside the **while** loop will never execute.

 Be careful when you are using the second syntax style (**do...while...**), because your code will execute at least one time, and this may or may not be the desired behavior.

For

The `for` loop logical construct is a little different from the series of `while` constructs that we just looked at in the logic it performs. You may have noticed in the samples in the previous section that the counter controlling the value of the `$repeat` variable has to be incremented manually with the `$repeat ++` command. With the `for` loop construct, the counter is built right into the conditional line, so the code for making the decision is a little more concise. Here is an example of the `for` looping structure that will do exactly the same thing as the `while` example shown previously:

```
for ($i = 0; $i <= 25; $i++) {
    echo "the counter is: " . $i . "<br/>" ;
}
```

The first part of this statement (`$i = 0`) sets the initial value for the loop, and the part after the semicolon is the portion of the statement that repeatedly tests to determine whether the code loop should be repeated. The final portion of the statement defines how the testing variable should be altered each time through. You can set the alteration value to anything that is logically valid. For example, you can increase it by 5 each time or you can decrease it by 12 if you like; it's up to you and the needs of the code where it is being written. With this construct, we have reduced the code from four lines to two. That's a 50 percent code reduction!

 I have changed the variable name from `$repeat` to `$i` to indicate iteration—this is a typical variable name used within the `for` loop. Using `$repeat` is still valid; it's just more compact to use a smaller variable name.

The `include`/`require` construct is discussed in the chapter on functions (Chapter 3) and `foreach` is discussed in the chapter on arrays (Chapter 5). Also, be sure to check out the chapter on the PHP version 5.3 features (Chapter 10), which covers a new control structure called `goto`.

Integration with Web Pages

One of the greatest features of PHP is that it gives you the ability to generate HTML based on integration with a web server, be that Apache, IIS, or any other leading web server. In this section, we will look at how PHP interacts with those web servers and where it can store its information while it is processing requests. Figure 2-2 shows the web server landscape and where each piece fits.

This is a simplistic view of how web servers work and where PHP fits into the mix. Today's websites seem so interactive with JavaScript and Ajax and other technologies helping out, but the reality is that websites are still *stateless*, meaning that one web page has no idea about any other web page—what was done on it, to it, or with it. They are

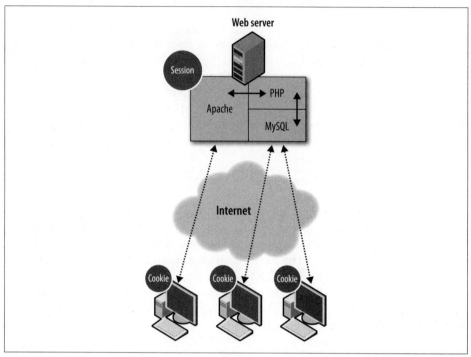

Figure 2-2. Basic web server with PHP configuration

completely independent of one another and, left alone, they cannot interact. However, you can store pieces of information within a web server's memory locations and retrieve that information at any time thereafter, as long as the data has not expired.

As shown in Figure 2-2, variable data can be stored for use from web page to web page or code file to code file in two main places: in *cookies* on the client side and in *sessions* on the server side. PHP is adept at working in both of these memory areas, and the next two sections explain their strengths and weaknesses in greater detail. We will then build on these concepts and discuss how PHP can leverage their power to great advantage.

Cookies

I am not a big fan of cookies. I hardly use them, but they do have their place. A cookie is merely a small file that the web server stores on the hard drive of the client's machine. Cookies have names (to identify them) and values. They can also have expiry, location, and security settings, but these settings are optional. The following code defines two cookies in PHP:

```
$data = "this will be placed in the cookie" ;
setcookie("CookieName", $data) ;
setcookie("AnotherCookieName", $data, time()+60*60*24*30) ;
```

The first `setcookie` command creates a cookie named "CookieName" on the client's machine and provides it with the contents of the `$data` variable. Since there is no expiry set, the cookie will cease to exist when the web session ends (when the browser is closed). That makes the second cookie creation statement (the one that creates "AnotherCookieName") self-explanatory: it is the same as in the previous example, except it has its own name and it has an expiry setting. The expiry setting is based on the UNIX epoch, so you should use either the `time()` or `mktime()` functions here.

 Since the cookie is stored on the client's machine, the expiry setting will be triggered based on that machine's internal time settings, not those of the web server.

The code above merely sets the value of the cookie on the client's machine. The other side of the equation is how to retrieve that data when you want it at some other point in your code or on some other page within your website. PHP has a series of system-wide variables that will appear quite often throughout this book, and they are collectively known as *superglobals*. They are, as the name implies, available to all scopes of a PHP script, be that functions, classes, or included external files. The first one of these superglobals that we will use has to do with retrieving the cookie value. Here is the code to retrieve the `AnotherCookieName` cookie we defined above:

```
$newData = $_COOKIE["AnotherCookieName"] ;
```

Superglobal variables are recognizable by their distinctive `$_` prefix and the fact that the remainder of the name is all in uppercase characters. In this case, `$_COOKIE` plainly makes reference to a value in the cookie array by the name of `AnotherCookieName`. This allows you to retrieve the value and use it anywhere you want as long as the cookie still exists (has not expired).

 It's always a good idea and a courtesy to set an expiry date and time when you are creating a cookie, or set it to 0 so it will expire when the browser is closed. Alternately, you can set the expiry date of a cookie to a value in the past; this will remove the cookie altogether (rather than waiting for a date in the future for it to expire). Removal of the cookie information from the client's computer where, in one sense, you are a guest is always the right thing to do. It's good to clean up after yourself.

Sessions

The alternative to cookies is the session entity. The session is essentially the same as the cookie, except that it resides on the web server and not the client's machine. This often has advantages in that the session is not dependent on the resources or settings of the client's machine, and thus tends to give you, the programmer, a bit more control. Sessions are stored in unique files on the server in a folder location as set by the `php.ini` directive `session.save_path`. There are quite a few session behavior settings in the *php.ini* file, so be sure to spend some time getting to know them if you really want your session management to be as efficient as possible. The following is an example of a session filename:

sess_p6lhj0ih6hte5ar8kqmge629a6

The filename starts with "sess_", followed by a random collection of letters and numbers. This allows PHP to keep track of the session instances on a server. The internals of that file are really just an associative array of key/value pairs and the life of the session is, generally speaking, as long as the time that the client's browser is open. To begin a session, however, you need to use the `session_start` function. If this is the first time that the function is being called during a period of web activity, this function creates the empty associative array on the web server; otherwise, the connection to the existing session is reestablished and the data within it is accessible. Here is a code example for starting a session and storing a value within:

```
session_start( );
$today = date("Y-m-d") ;  // load todays date in YYYY-MM-DD format
$_SESSION['today'] = $today ; // add that value into the session
$_SESSION['login_name'] = "Peter" ;  // add a session value for login name
```

Once the session is established, PHP knows about it and can handle its connection between file executions within the browser lifetime.

> The latest browsers have the capability of opening tabs within themselves and offering access to different web locations on each tab. If you open multiple tabs to the same web location, PHP treats that as one browser visit, so the session contents are shared across the tabs. This may lead to some unexpected results and activity.

If, on a subsequent page access during the same browser lifetime, you want to retrieve information from the existing session, all you have to do is reestablish the connection to the session and reference the array key that you are interested in, like this:

```
session_start () ;
$loginName = $_SESSION['login_name'] ;
echo $loginName . " is now logged in" ;
```

The `$_SESSION` superglobal array is really just a pivot point or holding cell for data that you want to preserve across pages in a website. You will find that there is much more control offered to you as a programmer by using session techniques rather than cookie techniques, because you are not at the potential mercy of the client's browser environment.

$_GET

The next superglobal entity to discuss is `$_GET`. The `$_GET` value is created automatically with the existence of a query string within a URL, or if a form is submitted with the

GET method (which still uses the URL as its vehicle). Any information that is sent along the query string in a key/value pair is subsequently loaded into the $_GET array in the called page.

   http://www.mynewwebsite.com/access.php?login=1&logname="Fred"

This URL example has two keys in the query string, one called login and the other called logname. When the *access.php* file is called, you can manipulate these values, if you so desire. All you have to do is reference the key within the associative array and then it's yours. Consider this code as part of the *access.php* file.

```
$login = $_GET['login'] ;
$logname = $_GET['logname'] ;
if ($login == 1) {
    echo "Welcome " . $logname ;
} else {
    echo "login failed... please try again " . $logname ;
}
```

The advantage to using the $_GET superglobal is that you can access information that is established on one page and use it in a called file.

 It's important to understand that the $_GET array is refreshed on each page call, so you have to pass it on to each page being called further down the call stack. It's different than the session concept in this regard.

$_POST

The $_POST superglobal array is almost identical to the $_GET array in that it can pass values effectively from one page to the next; the difference lies in the method of passing the information. The $_POST array does not use the query string in the URL of the called file as the transport method, but instead uses the server's Hypertext Transfer Protocol (HTTP) POST method. This is seen most often in submitted forms on web pages, but it can be used independently of the HTML <form> tag. Also, since it uses the POST method on the server and information is not sent as part of the URL, the information is less visible to the web user. So there is another modicum of security, even if it's not foolproof. The following code will use the <form> tag in a small web page and then show you how to manage the $_POST array in the called PHP file.

```
<html>
<head></head>
<body>
<form method='post' action='page2.php'>
please enter your name: <input type="text" size="15" name="fullname">
<input type=submit value="submit">
</form>
</body>
</html>
```

When the user clicks the submit button, *page2.php* is called. The code for this file follows:

```php
<?php
$name = $_POST['fullname'] ;
echo "the full name: " . $name ;
?>
<br/>
<a href="demo.php">back</a>
```

$_REQUEST

The final superglobal array that we will look at in this chapter is known as the *REQUEST* array. This is an all-inclusive array for each of the other requesting types of arrays, namely, $_COOKIE, $_GET, and $_POST. The drawback here is that each named key should be unique, otherwise $_REQUEST['lname'] could draw from any of the various arrays. Take a look at this code as an example:

```html
<html>
<head></head>
<body>
<?php setcookie('mname', 'Beck') ; ?>
<form method='post' action='page2.php?fname=peter&lname=smith'>
<input type="hidden" value="Simon" name="fname">
please enter your last name: <input type="text" size="15" name="lname">
<input type=submit value="submit">
</form>
</body>
</html>
```

This code sets a cookie, submits a form via the POST method, and when the form is posted, the code sends some values along the URL via the GET method. Now, chances are that you will not have code this diverse, but it is being shown here to demonstrate a possible stumbling block when using the REQUEST array. The <form> tag is calling *page2.php* as its action destination. Here is the code for that file:

```php
<?php
$fname = $_GET['fname'] ;
$lname = $_GET['lname'] ;
echo "the full name from GET: " . $fname . " " . $lname ;
$fname = $_POST['fname'] ;
$lname = $_POST['lname'] ;
echo "<br/>the full name from POST: " . $fname . " " . $lname ;
echo "<br/> the Request array -> " ;
var_dump($_REQUEST) ;
?>
<br/>
<a href="demo.php">back</a>
```

When this page is displayed, the following text is shown, assuming the user entered "MacIntyre" for the lname form input field.

the full name from GET: peter smith
the full name from POST: Simon MacIntyre
the Request array -> array(3) { ["fname"]=> string(5) "Simon" ["lname"]=> string(9) "MacIntyre"
["mname"]=> string(4) "Beck" }
back

As you can see, even though we have set the values in the GET and POST arrays differently, we have named the keys identically, so the REQUEST array by default gives precedence to the POST array. Also notice in this code that we didn't have to actually retrieve the cookie value from the first code listing—it is automatically forwarded to the REQUEST array when a subsequent file is called.

You can control the overall environment of superglobal arrays with the php.ini directive known as variables_order. The setting on my server is GPC. This means that the arrays are loaded and created in GET, POST, and COOKIE order, with the latter elements taking precedence over the former if they are similarly named. The "G" stands for GET, the "P" for POST, and the "C" is for cookie. If you remove one of the letters in GPC, save the .ini file and restart your server. The array represented by that letter will not be created in the superglobal space on the web server.

CHAPTER 3

Functions (Doing It Once)

PHP uses functions, much like any other programming language, and it certainly is to your advantage to get to know how to make the most of them.

PHP defines functions in two ways: those that return a value and those that do not. Functions should stand alone from other segments of code as much as possible. The rules for defining a function are fairly simple; you designate a function using its reserved word, giving it a unique name beginning with a letter or an underscore character, followed by any number of letters, underscores, or numbers. Round brackets (()) follow the function name—these are used to pass in any parameters that govern the function (more on that later). Finally, use curly braces ({}) to surround any code that is to be contained within the function.

Here is a sample function:

```
function MyFunction ( ) {
    echo "This is being displayed because MyFunction has been called" ;
}
```

There is a difference between defining a function and calling one into action. The code above merely defines the function called MyFunction; it does not call it or activate it. Here is some code defining the function and then calling it:

```
function MyFunction ( ) {
    echo "This is being displayed because MyFunction has been called" ;
}

MyFunction () ;
```

If you are not expecting any value to be returned, the code above will work fine. It will simply print the string, "This is being displayed because MyFunction has been called."

Parameter Passing

Let's look at a few more aspects of functions. Functions can accept values that are passed to them (*parameters*) and they can also return values, as we mentioned.

It is generally a best practice to have one way "into" a function—by calling it, as above—and one way "out" of it—by having it complete its defined work and either return a value or not. It is not good practice to have conditional return statements within a function, because, at the very least, it adds unnecessary complexity and is therefore more difficult to troubleshoot and debug.

When passing a value to a function, the names of the entities or expressions that are passed do not need to be similarly named to the placeholder variables that are receiving the values; the values are assigned by position in the parameter list. Here is some sample code with two differently defined functions that will help to illustrate these points:

```php
function MyList ($first, $second, $third ) {
    echo "here is first: " . $first . "<br/> ";
    echo "here is second: " . $second . "<br/> ";
    echo "and here is third: " . $third . "<br/>";
}

function AddThese($first, $second, $third) {
    $answer = $first + $second + $third ;
    return $answer ;
}

MyList ("Peter", "Chris", "Dean") ;
echo "<br/><br/>";

$first = 5 ;
$second = 34 ;
$third = 237 ;
$math = AddThese($first, $second, $third) ;
echo "$first,  $second, and $third add up to: " . $math ;
```

When you run this code through the browser, the output is as shown in Figure 3-1.

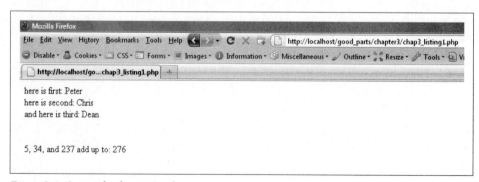

Figure 3-1. Output for function code

The first function, MyList, is passed three literal string values of people's first names. These are accepted into the function as three variables, namely $first, $second, and

$third. Once inside the function, they are merely echoed out onto the browser screen. No manipulation is done to these values within the function and nothing is returned back to the calling code.

The second function, AddThese, also accepts three values; in this case, they are numbers, but the definition of the function makes no distinction of that fact (the data type is not specified), so some assumptions are made in the code when the function is called. Three variables are assigned numerical values and they are sent to the function. The function does a calculation on these three entities and then returns the summation value to the calling code, which stores it in the variable called $math. No further manipulation of these three values is performed within the AddThese function.

Note that the variables named $first, $second, and $third only matter within each function. In a sense, there are two separate collections of variables called $first, $second, and $third, and they don't interfere with each other. As you can see by the output result, the values of $first, $second, and $third outside the function are not altered or affected by being sent into the AddThese function.

Default Parameters

Another aspect of defining functions is that you can give the parameters expected by the function (the *receiving parameters*) default values. This can lend strength to the function in the case that some of the parameters are not sent in. Consider the following variation on the AddThese function:

```
function AddThese($first = 5, $second = 10, $third = 15) {
    $answer = $first + $second + $third ;
    return $answer ;
}

$first = 5 ;
$second = 34 ;

$math = AddThese($first, $second) ;
echo "$first,  $second, and $third add up to: " . $math ;
```

This function call adds 5, 34, and whatever other number is required to total 54.

Essentially, when the AddThese function is called, the third parameter is not sent to the function. Since the definition of the function has default values assigned to its parameters, it will use those defaults when parameters are missing. So, you can actually build some forgiveness into your functions. In this case, the integer 15 is used as the third value, making the math is correct, although the displayed output text is misleading. The parameters in the receiving function are filled by position and, therefore, the calling line of code could be sending parameters named $forty and $fifty, and they would still be received as $first and $second.

Passing by Value Versus Passing by Reference

By default, all function parameters are passed to the function's code by their values only. This means that you can create a function that will accept a variable called $message, but pass it a variable by the name of $note. As long as the variables are in the same sequential position (both in calling the function and in execution of the function), the function will still work. In fact, even if the variables are named identically, they are treated as different variables and the function's variable name only exists (has scope) within that function. Take a look at the following simple example. Here, the variable named $message is passed to a function called displayit, and it is received into a function variable named $text. The value of the variable is passed to the function.

```
function displayit ($text) {
    echo $text ;
}
$message = "say hello to the web world";
displayit($message) ;
```

There may be situations in which you want both the value and the variable to be affected by a function's actions; in this case, you can pass variables to functions by reference (see Chapter 2). This tells PHP to pass the value of the variable to the function and at the same time extend the scope of that variable into the function so that when the function ends its work, any changes that were made to that variable will carry forward. For this to work, you have to precede the variable being passed by reference with an ampersand (&) character in the function's definition code. It still remains true that the variables in question are referred to by position. Here is an example of this in action:

```
function displayit (&$text) {
    $text .= ", you know you want to";
}
$message = "say hello to the web world";
displayit($message) ;
echo $message ;
```

The browser output of this code is shown in Figure 3-2.

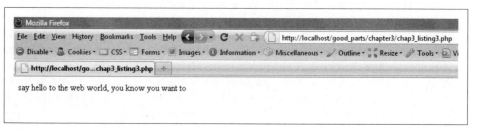

Figure 3-2. Browser output for functions by reference

Include and Require

Functions, by definition, are designed to be written once and used many times. Once you have created a function that you want to use in many code files, it would be a pain to have to copy that code into all the files in which you want to use it. PHP can insert the content of one code file into other code files, thus saving you the hassle of replication of code alterations in multiple locations. This is accomplished with the `include` and `require` statements (this is one of the flow control structures that was not discussed in Chapter 2). Once you have defined your function (or many functions) within a code file, called *my_functions.php* for example, you can instruct PHP to insert them into a different code file for use there.

You can use both the `include` and `require` statements to include the contents of a named file. The difference between them is that if the named file cannot be located with `include`, the code will continue to run, whereas with the `require` statement, if the named file cannot be located, the code will be stopped with a fatal error. In both cases, an error is raised if the file cannot be located, but it is only the `require` statement that fully stops the operation of the code.

Let's look at an example using the `displayit` function we defined in the previous section (saved in the file called *my_functions.php*) and the code that will be using that function (saved in another file, called *display_msg.php*).

```
###############
# my_functions.php file
###############
function displayit (&$text) {
    $text .= ", you know you want to";
}


###############
# display_msg.php file
###############

include "my_functions.php";

$message = "say hello to the web world";
displayit($message) ;
echo $message ;
```

If you need to update the `displayit` function later, you will only need to make changes in the *my_functions.php* file, not in many different files, even if the function code was replicated across many files.

PHP looks for files that are named for inclusion or requirement in a certain order. First, PHP looks for them in the location identified in the include_path settings within your *php.ini* file. If the file is not found there, PHP looks for it in the folder that contains the working code. You can, of course, name a fully defined path specifically for the file and thus not depend on any of these environmental settings.

Two other very similar statements exist in PHP, called include_once and require_once. These two statements work exactly the same way as their "regular" counterparts, except that they ensure the named file is only inserted into the file once, thus saving resources and potentially repeated insertions of the same code file.

Hopefully you can see from these small code examples that function libraries can be very valuable to PHP programmers once they are developed. This process of creating code once and reusing it many times is also used extensively in the object-oriented code paradigm, discussed in Chapter 6.

Built-In Functions Versus UDFs

So far you have been introduced to functions that you create yourself by writing code specifically for a defined custom purpose. These are called *user-defined functions* or UDFs. Additionally, PHP includes a plethora of predefined functions that you can use within your applications. There are functions for string manipulation, array management, database connectivity, date and time information, and so on. Be sure to check your PHP resources before you create functions that may already exist. Also, keep in mind that these native, or built-in, functions are always faster than ones you may build yourself, because they are highly optimized for use within PHP. Be aware, however, that some of these functions are very specific and therefore require dependent libraries to be added to the core of PHP. For MySQL database interaction, for example, you must add the MySQL library to the PHP environment before it will work at all.

CHAPTER 4

Strings

The string is one of the most widely used forms of web output. A string is simply a collection of text—letters, numbers, special characters, or a combination thereof. Strings can be manipulated, cut, trimmed, truncated, spliced, and concatenated with ease in PHP. We have already seen some examples of strings being sent out to the web browser in Chapters 1 and 2. In this chapter, we will spend a lot more time on the good parts of string manipulation.

String manipulation is important; think of all the websites you have visited this week and try to imagine how much of the content was text-based as opposed to image- or video-based. Even sites like YouTube and CNN are heavily dependent on text to ease communication with the visitor. So let's first see what a string actually consists of and how we can get that content onto a web browser.

What Is a String?

As mentioned above, a string is simply a collection of characters. These collections can be sent to the browser with either the `echo` or `print` PHP statements, but they have to be contained within defining markers (usually single or double quotations) for PHP to know which collection of characters you want displayed.

Although there is very little difference between echo and print (print returns a 1 when it has finished sending its output and takes only one parameter, whereas echo can take multiple parameters), I have made the choice to always use the echo command. You can execute the echo command with the short PHP tag and an equals sign (=) combination (if short_open_tag is turned on in the *php.ini* file, it's off by default generally), like this:

```
<?= "sending out some text" ; ?>.
```

It's really a personal choice as to which one to use, and I recommend that once you make that choice, stick with it so that your code remains consistent in this regard.

You Can Quote Me

Strings can be contained within either single or double quotation marks or a combination of the two, and in a HEREDOC or NOWDOC (more on these later). If you are building a string that will incorporate the contents of a variable, you are best served by using double quotes. Consider the following short code sample:

```
$fname = "Peter" ;
$lname = "MacIntyre" ;
$string = "The first name of the author of this book
is $fname and his last name is $lname";
echo $string ;
```

Here, in the creation of the $string variable, the code makes reference to two other variable names, and PHP *interpolates* (inserts) their contents. We can then echo out the $string variable. We can also accomplish this using single quotes, but we would have to do some concatenation with the period operator, because using single quotes do not allow for *variable expansion* (variable content insertion). The following code uses the single quote approach:

```
$fname = "Peter" ;
$lname = "MacIntyre" ;
$string = 'The first name of the author of this book is '
  . $fname . ' and his last name is ' . $lname ;
echo $string ;
```

The Great Escape

If you want to add the actual character of a double quote into the string, precede it with a backslash, like so:

```
$string = "He said \"go away\" to me" ;
```

This is known as *escaping* the character to the string. This keeps PHP from interpreting the second quotation mark as the end of the string. Alternately, you can use single quotes to contain the string, and accomplish exactly the same result:

```
$string = 'He said "go away" to me' ;
```

You can escape other characters with the use of a backslash. When using single-quote bookends, use the backslash to escape single quotes and backslashes (though these can become tricky to work with, for example, if you are trying to build a string of a folder path in Windows). Double-quote bookends allow you to escape a whole list of characters for special situations. For example, you can send the dollar sign ($) out to the browser by escaping it with a backslash when using double quotes so that PHP does not think that you are trying to send out the contents of a variable.

But be aware that you can use backslashes in other ways, too. For instance, the \n character combination is seen by PHP as a new line directive when written within a double-quoted string (this does not work the same way with single quotes). Check out the full list of these special escaped sequences at *http://www.php.net/manual/en/language.types.string.php*.

Again, you can also build strings with a combination of both single and double quotes; just be aware of the interpolative characteristics of the double quotes that the single quotes do not have. Also be aware of the new line directive within a string and how it is interpreted by double quotes and single quotes. When the new line directive (\n) is encased within a single quote string, it will not work, yet within double quotes it will. The following code snippet demonstrates this:

```
echo 'This sentence will not produce a new line \n';
echo "But this one will \n";
```

There is room for flexibility in the combinations of quotes that you can use, so be brave and experiment with them to see what you can accomplish.

Another way to build a string is to use a construct called HEREDOC. This construct is very similar to using double quotes in the sense that it interpolates variables, but it also lends itself to building longer strings, and therefore makes them more readable to the programmer. Begin the HEREDOC with three less than (<) signs followed by a name designation for the string being built. After the string is complete, repeat the name designation on its own line with a terminating semicolon. Here is an example:

```
$string = <<< RightHERE
Lorem ipsum dolor sit amet, consectetur adipiscing elit.
Fusce eget nisl a metus rhoncus placerat ac ac nisl.
Fusce consectetur tempus "tincidunt. Proin congue
dapibus neque", at congue lectus volutpat in.
Duis commodo, est tempor aliquam molestie, odio dolor fringilla arcu,
nec iaculis est libero vitae erat.
RightHERE;

echo $string ;
```

The output of the above HEREDOC code sample is shown in Figure 4-1.

Figure 4-1. Sample HEREDOC browser output

You will find that the use of the HEREDOC construct lends itself very well to building Structured Query Language (SQL) statements. This technique will be used extensively in Chapter 7, where we discuss databases.

As you can see, there are many ways in which to define strings, and there are equally as many ways in which to manipulate them. Keep in mind that strings can also be handed to your code as opposed to you building them manually. Strings of alphanumeric text—arrays, first names, last names, phone numbers, part codes, email addresses, and so on—can be passed into a code file for processing by way of a form field, via the `$_POST` or `$_GET` methods (see Chapter 2).

String Functions (Best of)

For the rest of this chapter, let's look at the best and most useful string functions in PHP so that you will have the tools to manage most of what you will have to deal with. I have grouped these functions into semilogical categories and given code samples for most of them. In many of the examples, we will be looking for the proverbial needle in a haystack—the needle being the string we are looking for with each function, and the haystack being the overall content in which we are performing each operation.

You will notice that many of the functions we are about to look at in the next few chapters do not necessarily follow a common style or naming convention. This is mostly a result of PHP being an open source product that many people and many years have affected, but is also caused by things like some functions being named after the C++ equivalents they are based upon. Sometimes you will see functions defined with underscores, like `strip_tags`, while a similar function is named without them, such as `stripslashes`. This flexibility is simultaneously a strength and a weakness of PHP.

String Trimmings

Strings are often passed around in code with either leading or trailing whitespace. To make sure your strings are not carrying this extra content, simply use the `ltrim` or

---

`rtrim` functions (if you know which end of the string has the extra content). If you want to be sure to get the whitespace content from both ends of the string at the same time, use the `trim` function. Here is a sample:

```
$string = "     The quick brown fox jumps over the lazy dog     " ;
var_dump(ltrim($string));
echo "<br/>";
var_dump(rtrim($string));
echo "<br/>";
var_dump(trim($string));
```

The output of this code is:

```
string(48) "The quick brown fox jumps over the lazy dog     "
string(48) "     The quick brown fox jumps over the lazy dog"
string(43) "The quick brown fox jumps over the lazy dog"
```

 We are using the function **var_dump** here for producing output, because there is more information returned with this function than simply echoing or printing the output to the browser.

There are five spaces on either side of the text string, so you can see that the first two trimmings are being reported as having the same length, 48 characters, yet there is space remaining on the end of the first output and space remaining on the front of the second output. When we use `trim`, the space is removed from both the front and the end of this sample string, yielding a result with only 43 characters.

When you are truly hunting a needle in a haystack, you can also use the `trim` function to return a "needle" of supplied characters that are to be trimmed out of the string, as in the following:

```
$string = "The quick brown fox jumps over the lazy dog" ;
var_dump(trim($string, "Thedog"));
```

With the following output:

```
string(37) " quick brown fox jumps over the lazy "
```

The `trim` function looks at both ends of the string for the supplied characters and strips them out. Notice that the spaces remain at the beginning and the end of this string, which is a slight variation in functionality when the second argument, specifying the characters to be stripped, is supplied to the `trim` function. This behavior is also true for the `ltrim` and the `rtrim` functions. If you want the spaces trimmed as well, you will need to specify them.

Character Case Management

The next grouping of string functions can manipulate the capitalization of portions of a supplied string. Using the same sample string of text, we can affect the initial case of each word within the string with the `ucwords` function, as shown here:

```
$string = "The quick brown fox jumps over the lazy dog" ;
var_dump ucwords($string) ;
```

The expected output is:

string(43) "The Quick Brown Fox Jumps Over The Lazy Dog"

You can manipulate the case of an entire string with the `strtoupper` and the `strto lower` functions. These functions turn the entire string to uppercase and lowercase characters, respectively. Look at this code and the resulting output:

```
$string = "The quick brown fox jumps over the lazy dog" ;
var_dump( strtoupper($string)) ;
echo "<br/>" ;
var_dump( strtolower($string)) ;
```

string(43) "THE QUICK BROWN FOX JUMPS OVER THE LAZY DOG"
string(43) "the quick brown fox jumps over the lazy dog"

The next two functions are probably not as widely used as the previous functions, yet they do have their place, especially in manipulating content being saved from web form pages. The `ucfirst` and `lcfirst` functions change just the first character of a string to uppercase and lowercase, respectively. This can be very useful in handling data like a last name that you want to ensure has a leading uppercase letter. Here is some sample code:

```
$string = "smith" ;
var_dump( ucfirst ($string)) ;
echo "<br/>" ;
$string = "SMITH" ;
var_dump( lcfirst($string)) ;
```

The expected output is:

string(5) "Smith"
string(5) "sMITH"

 `lcfirst` is available only in PHP 5.3 and later.

String Content Searching

You will almost certainly be doing more content manipulation than just playing with the cases of your text strings, so here we will look at additional ways to alter the contents of a string and to look for that proverbial "needle."

The first thing we'll look at here allows us to count the size of a string. This can come in handy if you are trying to enter data into a database field that only takes a set number of characters, for instance. There are two functions in this group: first is `str_word_count`, which, as expected, counts the number of words in a given string. Second, `strlen` returns the length of the provided string. Careful, though—strlen counts spaces as part of the length of the string as well, so you may want to trim a string before you ask for its length. Here is some sample code:

```
$string = "  The quick brown fox jumps over the lazy dog" ;
echo "word count: " . str_word_count($string) ;
echo "<br/>" ;
echo "String length: " . strlen($string) ;
echo "<br/>" ;
echo "String length trimmed: " . strlen(trim($string)) ;
```

The expected output is:

```
Word count: 9
String length: 45
String length trimmed: 43
```

We can also ask PHP to query the provided string to see if a specific portion of text (subset) is contained within it. There are two functions for doing this. The first, `strstr`, is case-sensitive, while the second, `stristr`, will search irrespective of case. Both of these functions will look through the haystack for the specified needle and, if they find it, will return the portion of the string from the beginning of the needle to the end of the haystack. If the needle is not found, `false` is returned. Here is some code that demonstrates this:

```
$string = "The quick brown fox jumps over the lazy dog" ;
$needle = "BROWN fox";
echo "strstr: " ;
var_dump( strstr($string, $needle) );
echo "<br/>" ;
echo "stristr: " ;
var_dump(stristr($string, $needle) );
echo "<br/>" ;
$needle = "the" ;
echo "strstr: " ;
var_dump( strstr($string, $needle) );
echo "<br/>" ;
echo "stristr: " ;
var_dump(stristr($string, $needle) );
```

```
strstr: bool(false)
strstr: string(33) "brown fox jumps over the lazy dog"
strstr: string(12) "the lazy dog"
strstr: string(43) "The quick brown fox jumps over the lazy dog"
```

The first attempt returns `false` since the capitalized word "BROWN" is not in the provided string. But when we search for it irrespective of case by using `stristr`, we get the expected result. In the second grouping, we change the needle to "the" and the resulting output is also as expected: with case sensitivity, the output begins at the first lowercase "the" and, without it, the output begins at the beginning.

Next is a collection of functions that can find positions, manipulate content, and extract needles from the haystack. You can pinpoint the location of a needle (the content you are looking for) within the haystack (a string) by using the `strpos` function. If the specified string is not found at all, `strpos` will return false. This is not the same as a returned 0, so be sure to test your returned values with = = = (triple equals test) to ensure accuracy within you results. You can replace a subset of text within a string with the `str_replace` function. Finally, you can extract a subset of text from within the haystack into another variable with the `substr` function. Some of these functions work best together. For example, you might find the starting position of a needle with `strpos` and then, in the same line of code, extract the contents for a set number of characters to another variable with the `substr` function. Consider this sample code and its subsequent output:

```
$string = "The quick brown fox jumps over the lazy dog" ;
$position = strpos($string, "fox");
echo "position of 'fox' $position <br/>" ;
$result = substr($string, strpos($string, "fox"), 8);
echo "8 characters after finding the position of 'fox': $result <br/>" ;
$new_string = str_replace("the", "black", $string);
echo $new_string;


position of 'fox' 16
8 characters after finding the position of 'fox': fox jump
The quick brown fox jumps over black lazy dog
```

String Modification

Another valuable collection of functions includes those that can alter a string of HTML content. The `strip_tags` function removes embedded HTML tags from within a string. There is also a condition to the function that allows us to retain a list of allowable tags. Here is an example:

```
$string = "The <strong>quick</strong> brown fox <a href='jumping.php'>jumps</a>
over the lazy dog" ;
echo $string . "<br/>" ;
echo strip_tags($string) . "<br/>" ;
echo strip_tags($string, '<strong>') ;
```

The browser output will look like this:

The **quick** brown fox *jumps* over the lazy dog
The quick brown fox jumps over the lazy dog
The **quick** brown fox jumps over the lazy dog

And if you reveal the source of the displayed browser page, you will see this:

```
The <strong>quick</strong> brown fox <a href='jumping.php'>jumps</a>
over the lazy dog<br/>

The quick brown fox jumps over the lazy dog<br/>

The <strong>quick</strong> brown fox jumps over the lazy dog
```

Note that the tags are completely removed from the string in the second display and all tags except `<strong>` are removed from the third display.

The next two string functions can be thought of as a pair of opposites, in that one reverses what the other accomplishes, depending on how they are used. They are `addslashes` and `stripslashes`. If you read "The Great Escape" on page 34, you'll remember that you can escape some special characters like the double quote or the backslash by using a preceding backslash. The `addslashes` function looks for those special characters in the provided string and escapes them with an added backslash. The reversal of that is accomplished with `stripslashes`. Sample code follows:

```
$web_path = "I'm Irish and my name is O'Mally" ;
echo addslashes($web_path) . "<br/>" ;
echo stripslashes($web_path) ;
```

I\'m Irish and my name is O\'Mally
I'm Irish and my name is O'Mally

 If you are using `addslashes` to escape a preexisting backslash, and then using the `stripslashes` function on that same string, all backslashes will be stripped out. This may not be what you want.

HTML, as you probably know, is heavily dependent on markup tags for displaying items, and sometimes these tags are better served in what I like to call their "raw" state. For example, the less-than sign (<) can be represented in HTML as <, a greater-than sign (>) as >, the ampersand (&) as &, and so on. With the use of the `htmlentities` function, we can convert the contents of a supplied string containing these characters to their "raw" state. This is often used for security reasons when accepting data from an outside source into a web system. If desired, we can reverse the effect with the `html_entity_decode` function. Here is a sample:

```
$string = "The <strong>quick</strong> brown fox <a href='jumping.php'>jumps
</a> over the lazy dog" ;
```

```
echo htmlentities($string) . "<br/>" ;
echo html_entity_decode($string) ;
```

```
The &lt;strong&gt;quick&lt;/strong&gt; brown fox &lt;a
href='jumping.php'&gt;jumps&lt;/a&gt; over the lazy dog<br/>
The <strong>quick</strong> brown fox <a href='jumping.php'>jumps</a> over the lazy
dog
```

This can be very useful in the case of someone commenting on a blog entry or signing a website guest book, for example. The supplied text can be intercepted, preventing it from containing any potentially actionable HTML markup, as all HTML is converted to "raw" nonworking entities.

There are two more string functions that I want to bring to your attention, and these have great application in the security aspect of web development when dealing with passwords. The first is `str_shuffle`, which makes a random reorganization of a supplied string. You can use this function if you want to have PHP generate a randomly arranged string from a supplied string (to make a password a little more difficult to guess, for example). Alternately, you can use the MD5 function to really scramble up a supplied string. The MD5 function is used to get a 32-bit hexadecimal equivalent of the supplied string.

 MD5 always returns the same hash result for a given string, while `str_shuffle` randomly reorganizes the string contents each time, so for extra security you could randomize the string and then perform MD5 on it.

Here is some code with these functions in action:

```
$string = "The quick brown fox jumps over the lazy dog" ;
echo str_shuffle($string) . "<br/>" ;
echo md5($string) . "<br/>" ;
echo md5(str_shuffle($string)) ;
```

Initial display in the browser produces this output:

```
dhuo p qr xnus hzeyveloftaiewbTojrg mock
9e107d9d372bb6826bd81d3542a419d6
f71d7b9a5880c06163ed8adbdee5b55e
```

Refreshing the browser gives this output:

```
ugn uiferlwckvxT thzrbh o mqo doeaoesjp y
9e107d9d372bb6826bd81d3542a419d6
1356809b12da9a25482891606ccfaa8f
```

The second line of output, the single use of MD5, does not change on a page refresh, while the other content does.

 There is more detailed discussion on the MD5 function (and its more secure cousin sha1) in Chapter 9 on security.

PHP provides many more string functions, and over time you may choose to become familiar with many of them. The string functions we have covered here are those that you are likely to find the most beneficial right away. In the next chapter, we will follow a similar pattern with a discussion of arrays.

CHAPTER 5

Arrays

Now that we have a handle on the concept of strings, let's take a look at the power and flexibility of arrays. Arrays are known as *compound data types*; all that really means is that they are more complex in structure than simple strings and integers, which are also known as *scalar data types*. Imagine an array as an egg carton. It carries 12 individual compartments that can house one egg each, yet it travels around as one entity. The compartments can be broken off and made into single egg holders, or holders in any number combination. Additionally, these compartments are not limited to holding only eggs; they can hold rocks, or cookies, or match sticks. Of course, an analogy like this has its limitations—egg cartons cannot easily be expanded and they cannot hold other egg cartons, all of which, we will see, arrays are excellent at doing.

Let's talk more precisely about arrays. Like egg cartons, arrays have compartments (*elements*) that hold data. The elements and their respective data always travel together (although you can have an empty element without data) and are known as *key/value pairs*. So, if we had an array of five elements, each containing a number in the range from 1 to 5, it would look like Table 5-1 (elements start their counting with 0).

Table 5-1. Visual representation of an array with numeric (indexed) keys

Keys	0	1	2	3	4
Values	1	2	3	4	5

Indexed Arrays

Arrays with numerical keys are known as *indexed arrays*. The keys can also be named with strings, if you prefer, creating what is known as an *associative array*, as you will see later in this chapter. Let's consider an array called $myArray.

 Array variable names follow the same naming rules as regular PHP variables (see the section "Variables: Data Types, Loose Typing, and Scope" on page 9).

In PHP code, you can reference the elements of an array by their keys, surrounded by square brackets. If we want to take the value of the third element of the array—the contents being the number 3 in this case—and assign it to its own variable, the code would look like this:

```
// remember, the elemets of the array start with 0
$singleValue = $myArray[2] ;  echo $singleValue ;  // output would be 3
```

Now, this assumes that we have already defined the array somewhere else in our code. There are two ways in which to create arrays; the first is a variation on the use of the square bracket syntax. Here is the code for creating an array with this method:

```
$myArray[0] = 1 ;
$myArray[1] = 2 ;
$myArray[2] = 3 ;
$myArray[3] = 4 ;
$myArray[] = 5 ;
```

This method assumes that we already know the key order and their values, as the key numbers here are hardcoded. Notice that the last line of code in the above example is not "forcing" the key number inside the square brackets; when this is done (not providing the key number), the result is that the next available integer key will be assigned to that element for us.

Creating an array in this fashion may or may not be what you want. The other method available is to use the **array** function with the key/value pairs passed together and separated by commas, like so:

```
$myArray = array(0 => 1, 1 => 2, 2 => 3, 3 => 4, 4 => 5) ;
```

This way of creating an array is much more condensed, yet it may be a little more difficult for humans to read.

If you want to create an empty array, just use the array function without any parameters:

```
$a = array()
```

The keys of any array have to be named uniquely, otherwise there would be confusion when referencing their contents. PHP won't prevent you from using the same key multiple times in an assignment, but each identical key assigned will replace the one before it.

Associative Arrays

So far we have looked at indexed arrays, but as I mentioned before, the key portion of an array can also consist of character strings. The data values that we have looked at so far have also been numerical, but these too can be changed to string data, as shown in Table 5-2.

Table 5-2. Visual representation of an array with named (associative) keys

Keys	first	second	fname	initial	lname
Values	1	2	Peter	B	MacIntyre

To create the array represented in Table 5-2, use the same code syntax options as before, but with appropriate alterations for the strings:

```
$myArray['first'] = 1 ;
$myArray['second'] = 2 ;
$myArray['fname'] = "Peter" ;
$myArray['initial'] = "B" ;
$myArray['lname'] = "MacIntyre" ;
```

Alternately, you can use the following:

```
$myArray = array('first' => 1, 'second' => 2,
'fname' => "Peter", 'initial' => "B", 'lname' => "MacIntyre") ;
```

There is no real difference here between the use of single or double quotes, and as you can see, they are interchangeable. Just be careful with them when escaping special characters or variable contents in the same way you would with regular string management (see "The Great Escape" on page 34).

You can reference the array's elements the same as you would an indexed array, again using the string instead of a number. So, if you want to echo out your full name using the contents of this array, write the following code (with some string formatting added in for clarity):

```
echo $myArray['fname'] . " " . $myArray['initial']
    . " " . $myArray['lname'] ;
```

Arrays from Another Dimension

The data types that can be held within the elements of arrays are the same as those that can be held within a regular variable: integers, strings, dates, Booleans, and so on. One really great thing about arrays, though, is that their elements can also hold other arrays, thus making them multidimensional. There is no limit to the depth arrays' dimensions, but after about three levels, it can become difficult to keep the elements and their keys straight. Here is some code showing a two-dimensional array:

```
$myArray['first'] = 1 ;
$myArray['fruit'] = array("Apples", "Oranges", "Tomato") ;
$myArray['fname'] = "Peter" ;
$myArray['initial'] = "B" ;
$myArray['lname'] = "MacIntyre" ;

var_dump($myArray);
```

It's a good idea to familiarize yourself with two-dimensional arrays, as they are the main structural representation of database results. More on that in Chapter 7.

To make reference to the elements of a second (or deeper) dimension, just continue with the square brackets concept. To refer to the element in our example that contains the string "Tomato," do this:

```
echo $myArray['fruit'][2] ;
```

Remember that the elements are counted beginning with zero, so you will need to ask for element 2 to get the third one. This is true even though we assigned strings to both the keys and the values. And yes, a tomato is a fruit!

Arrays Can Be Dynamic

As you have probably already realized, arrays in PHP are dynamic. This means that with the use of the right code commands and functions, you can add elements to an existing array without much effort. You can also delete elements from an array just as easily. In fact, you can do a lot of things to arrays (more of which we will examine later in this chapter), but for now let's just look at adding to and taking away from them.

To add an element to the end of an existing array, simply use the empty square brackets approach.

If you are adding to the end of an associative array and fail to provide a key, PHP will add the element with the next highest index value, thus making a mixed index and associative array.

Let's look at some code:

```
$myArray = array('first' => 1, 'second' => 2,
'fname' => "Peter", 'initial' => "B", 'lname' => "MacIntyre") ;

echo $myArray['fname'] . " " . $myArray['initial']
     . " " . $myArray['lname'] ;
echo "<br/>" ;
$myArray[] = "555-5678" ;
var_dump($myArray) ;
```

Here, we add a new value (a phone number) to the end of the array, but because we do not provide a key, when we var_dump the array we get output showing that the last element in the array has the key of 0, which is the next numerical index value in this particular array. If we want to avoid this behavior, we simply add an associative key to the command ($myArray["phone"] = "555-5678" ;) :

Peter B MacIntyre
array(6) { ["first"]=> int(1) ["second"]=> int(2) ["fname"]=> string(5) "Peter"
["initial"]=> string(1) "B" ["lname"]=> string(9) "MacIntyre" [0]=> string(8) "555-5678"
}

One option for removing an element from an array is the **array_splice** function. This is a very powerful function with a number of different options, so be sure to look more deeply into its use with the help of the php.net website (*http://php.net/index.php*). Here, we just want to remove the last element of the array: the phone number element that we added before. To do that, we can write code like this:

```
$myArray = array('first' => 1, 'second' => 2,
'fname' => "Peter", 'initial' => "B",
'lname' => "MacIntyre", 'phone' => "555-5678") ;

var_dump($myArray) ;
echo "<br/>" ;
array_splice($myArray, 4);
var_dump($myArray) ;
```

The result of **var_dump** on the array now looks like this:

array(6) { ["first"]=> int(1) ["second"]=> int(2) ["fname"]=> string(5) "Peter"
["initial"]=> string(1) "B" ["lname"]=> string(9) "MacIntyre" ["phone"]=> string(8)
"555-5678" }
array(5) { ["first"]=> int(1) ["second"]=> int(2) ["fname"]=> string(5) "Peter"
["initial"]=> string(1) "B" ["lname"]=> string(9) "MacIntyre" }

The first option in the **array_splice** function is the array to be worked on, and the second option is the array position with which to start the work. In this case, we are telling PHP to remove the fifth element from this array. Notice that we are using the index position value here, 4, and not the key value of 0. You can use a conditional third option, length, which indicates how many elements this work should be performed on. Since our code does not use this option, the default action is to perform the task on the last element of the array. If you want to maintain the original array and make a new one that will hold the result of the **array_splice** function, simply assign the result to a new variable and **array_splice** will create a completely new array for you. We can change the code to remove all the contents of the array that have to do with my name and place them into a new array with the following code:

```
$myArray = array('first' => 1, 'second' => 2,
'fname' => "Peter", 'initial' => "B",
'lname' => "MacIntyre", 'phone' => "555-5678") ;

$name_array = array_splice($myArray, 2, 3);
var_dump($myArray) ;
echo "<br/>" ;
var_dump($name_array) ;
```

The output would be thus:

```
array(3) { ["first"]=> int(1) ["second"]=> int(2) ["phone"]=> string(8) "555-5678" }
array(3) { ["fname"]=> string(5) "Peter" ["initial"]=> string(1) "B" ["lname"]=> string(9)
"MacIntyre" }
```

Notice here, too, that the `array_splice` function leaves the phone number as the last element in $myArray, effectively lifting out the elements that have to do with the name. This is accomplished with the third option (the limit option) in the `array_splice` function.

Another way to manipulate arrays in this fashion is to use the `unset` function. It is actually more efficient and a little simpler to use than `array_splice`. If we want to remove the middle initial from the array above, we would code the following to remove it from the array:

```
unset($myArray['initial']) ;
```

Traversing Arrays

Before we get into the listing of the best array functions, we need to look at ways to easily walk through, or traverse, an array. If you read Chapter 2, you might remember that we skipped over a flow control structure and put it on the shelf until this chapter. That flow control structure is the `foreach` construct, and it has great value and use in the context of arrays. It will allow you to step through each element of a supplied array and implement almost any code on the key/value pairs. In addition, this construct will place the key and value of each iteration into their own variables. Using our array sample from before, let's go through each key/value pair and echo each one out onto the screen. We can do that with this code:

```
$myArray = array('first' => 1, 'second' => 2,
'fname' => "Peter", 'initial' => "B",
'lname' => "MacIntyre", 'phone' => "555-5678") ;

foreach ($myArray as $key => $value) {
    echo "the Key is: " . $key . " and its value is: " . $value . "<br/>";
}
```

And the produced output is like this:

```
the Key is: first and its value is: 1
the Key is: second and its value is: 2
the Key is: fname and its value is: Peter
the Key is: initial and its value is: B
the Key is: lname and its value is: MacIntyre
the Key is: phone and its value is: 555-5678
```

If you are only interested in the values of the array, you can still use the `foreach` construct and leave out the key portion: `foreach ($myArray as $value)`. It will ignore the key portion of the element and provide you with just the corresponding values. Alternately, if you are only interested in the key portion of the array, you can write code like this to work within a foreach loop:

```
foreach(array_keys($a) as $key);
```

Array Functions (Best of)

Arrays are so versatile and so widely used that there are very many built-in PHP functions you can employ. Here, I will once again pick out the best and most effective of these functions and show them to you in code.

Sorting Arrays

Arrays can be organized and reorganized in many ways, primarily through the family of sort functions. Some of these sorting functions are best suited to working on associative arrays, and some to indexed arrays, and we will see the difference here in the example code. The sort function sorts the array based on the values in it, and reissues keys sequentially once the sorting is complete. The rsort function does exactly the same thing, except that the sorting is done in reverse order. The asort and arsort functions do the same sorting based on the array values, but retain the original key settings. Finally, ksort and krsort perform their sorting processes on the keys of a provided array (it naturally makes the most sense to use these with an associative array, since an indexed array generally already has sorted keys). The following is some sample code that shows all these sorting functions in action.

 I am a huge fan of the rock band Genesis, so the following code examples are my tribute to the fact that they have finally been inducted into the Rock and Roll Hall of Fame!

```
$ClassicGenesis = array("Tony Banks", "Phil Collins","Mike Rutherford",
"Steve Hackett","Peter Gabriel" ) ;

sort ($ClassicGenesis) ;
echo "<strong>Sorted on Values with re-generated Keys:</strong> <br/>";
foreach ($ClassicGenesis as $key => $value) {
    echo "the Key is: " . $key . " and its value is: " . $value . "<br/>";
}
$ClassicGenesis = array("Tony Banks", "Phil Collins","Mike Rutherford",
"Steve Hackett","Peter Gabriel" ) ;
rsort ($ClassicGenesis) ;
echo "<strong>Now sorted in reverse order on Values with re-generated
Keys: </strong><br/>";
foreach ($ClassicGenesis as $key => $value) {
    echo "the Key is: " . $key . " and its value is: " . $value . "<br/>";
}
$ClassicGenesis = array("Tony Banks", "Phil Collins","Mike Rutherford",
"Steve Hackett","Peter Gabriel" ) ;
```

```
asort ($ClassicGenesis) ;
echo "<strong>Now sorted in order of Values with Keys intact:</strong><br/>";
foreach ($ClassicGenesis as $key => $value) {
    echo "the Key is: " . $key . " and its value is: " . $value . "<br/>";
}
$ClassicGenesis = array("Tony Banks", "Phil Collins","Mike Rutherford",
"Steve Hackett","Peter Gabriel" ) ;
arsort ($ClassicGenesis) ;
echo "<strong>Now sorted in reverse order of Values with Keys
 intact: </strong><br/>";
foreach ($ClassicGenesis as $key => $value) {
    echo "the Key is: " . $key . " and its value is: " . $value . "<br/>";
}

$ClassicGenesis = array("Keyboards" => "Tony Banks", "Drums" => "Phil Collins",
"Bass Guitar" =>"Mike Rutherford","Lead Guitar" => "Steve Hackett",
"Vocals" =>"Peter Gabriel" ) ;
ksort ($ClassicGenesis) ;
echo "<strong>Now sorted in order based on Keys: </strong><br/>";
foreach ($ClassicGenesis as $key => $value) {
    echo "the Key is: " . $key . " and its value is: " . $value . "<br/>";
}

$ClassicGenesis = array("Keyboards" => "Tony Banks", "Drums" => "Phil Collins",
"Bass Guitar" =>"Mike Rutherford","Lead Guitar" => "Steve Hackett",
"Vocals" =>"Peter Gabriel" ) ;
krsort ($ClassicGenesis) ;
echo "<strong>Now sorted in reverse order based on Keys: </strong><br/>";
foreach ($ClassicGenesis as $key => $value) {
    echo "the Key is: " . $key . " and its value is: " . $value . "<br/>";
}
```

I recreated the array each time for clarity because the sorting functions all reorder the existing array with the newly reorganized keys and values; I therefore would be using the altered array if it weren't reset to its original values each time. These functions return a true or false depending on success or failure.

The output of the above code is:

Sorted on values with regenerated keys:

the Key is: 0 and its value is: Mike Rutherford
the Key is: 1 and its value is: Peter Gabriel
the Key is: 2 and its value is: Phil Collins
the Key is: 3 and its value is: Steve Hackett
the Key is: 4 and its value is: Tony Banks

Now sorted in reverse order on values with regenerated keys:

the Key is: 0 and its value is: Tony Banks
the Key is: 1 and its value is: Steve Hackett
the Key is: 2 and its value is: Phil Collins

the Key is: 3 and its value is: Peter Gabriel
the Key is: 4 and its value is: Mike Rutherford

Now sorted in order of values with keys intact:

the Key is: 2 and its value is: Mike Rutherford
the Key is: 4 and its value is: Peter Gabriel
the Key is: 1 and its value is: Phil Collins
the Key is: 3 and its value is: Steve Hackett
the Key is: 0 and its value is: Tony Banks

Now sorted in reverse order of values with keys intact:

the Key is: 0 and its value is: Tony Banks
the Key is: 3 and its value is: Steve Hackett
the Key is: 1 and its value is: Phil Collins
the Key is: 4 and its value is: Peter Gabriel
the Key is: 2 and its value is: Mike Rutherford

Now sorted in order based on keys:

the Key is: Bass Guitar and its value is: Mike Rutherford
the Key is: Drums and its value is: Phil Collins
the Key is: Keyboards and its value is: Tony Banks
the Key is: Lead Guitar and its value is: Steve Hackett
the Key is: Vocals and its value is: Peter Gabriel

Now sorted in reverse order based on keys:

the Key is: Vocals and its value is: Peter Gabriel
the Key is: Lead Guitar and its value is: Steve Hackett
the Key is: Keyboards and its value is: Tony Banks
the Key is: Drums and its value is: Phil Collins
the Key is: Bass Guitar and its value is: Mike Rutherford

Another great sorting function in PHP is usort. This function allows you to sort an array based on specific criteria that you define. It allows you to define a comparison function that is called repeatedly for each element in the provided array, comparing it to its neighbor elements. Be sure to look into this function if you have an array sorting need that is not met by the other, more basic ones.

Math-Type Functions

There are two handy math-type functions that you can perform on arrays. These, naturally, lend themselves to indexed arrays and numerical values. The first one to look at is the `array_sum` function, which simply adds up the values of the array elements and returns that answer to a variable.

The other math-type function is called **count** which, as the name implies, merely counts and returns the number of elements in the array. Here in the sample code, we use both functions to generate the average of some test grades, with the output following:

```
$grades = array(87,88,98,74,56,94,67) ;

$addedGrades = array_sum($grades);
echo "The sum of the provided grades is: $addedGrades <br/>";
$avgGrades = array_sum($grades) / count($grades) ;
echo "and the average of these grades is: " . round($avgGrades,2) ;
```

The sum of the provided grades is: 564
The average of these grades is: 80.57

This code also uses the **round** function to clean up the display of the average value and keep it to two decimal places.

Array Potpourri

Now let's look at some other array functions that are essentially unique in their functionality and are therefore somewhat difficult to group together. I will describe each function and how it works, then give some sample code and output. I will combine some of them into the same code listing where it can be done in order to save space (and trees).

If you want to make sure all the elements in a provided array are unique, use the `array_unique` function. This function identifies and removes any duplication in an array and shrinks the array if there are in fact duplicate values. The element keys are not renumbered when this function is complete.

If you want to determine whether a value exists within a provided array, use the `in_array` function. This function looks for the provided portion of data within the array in question and returns true or false accordingly. If you want the value returned or separated out of the array—as opposed to the basic Boolean response that `in_array` provides—use the `array_search` function.

If you want to randomize the values of an array, use the `shuffle` function. This takes the provided array and randomly reorders the values while keeping the keys in their sequential order.

If you want to take a random key or keys out of a provided array, use the `array_rand` function. If you only want one random key, it will be returned to a variable with the data type of the key's value (indexed or associative); if you request more than one random value from an array, the result will be another array.

Here is some sample code using all the functions mentioned so far, followed by its corresponding output:

```
$grades = array(87,88,98,74,56,94,67,98,49) ;

var_dump($grades);
echo "<br/>" ;
$uniqueGrades = array_unique($grades);
var_dump($uniqueGrades);
echo "<br/>" ;

if (in_array(49, $grades) ) {
    echo "there is a 49 in here and it is at element: " . array_search(49, $grades) ;
} else {
    echo "no 49s here" ;
}
echo "<br/>" ;
shuffle($grades) ;
var_dump($grades);
echo "<br/>" ;

$random = array_rand($grades);
echo "the random key from grades is: " . $random ;
```

```
array(9) { [0]=> int(87) [1]=> int(88) [2]=> int(98) [3]=> int(74) [4]=> int(56) [5]=>
int(94) [6]=> int(67) [7]=> int(98) [8]=> int(49) }
array(8) { [0]=> int(87) [1]=> int(88) [2]=> int(98) [3]=> int(74) [4]=> int(56) [5]=>
int(94) [6]=> int(67) [8]=> int(49) }
there is a 49 in here and it is at element: 8
array(9) { [0]=> int(87) [1]=> int(56) [2]=> int(98) [3]=> int(67) [4]=> int(98) [5]=>
int(74) [6]=> int(88) [7]=> int(49) [8]=> int(94) }
the random key from grades is: 4
```

If you want to convert all your array elements into separate variables with the keys as the variable names and the values transferred into those variables, use the **extract** function. This is best used on associative arrays, since a variable named $0 or $1 is not valid in PHP.

 Be careful that the elements you are extracting do not have key names that may overwrite other variables in your code—this can also be a security concern when the function is applied to untrusted input, because it may allow the input to overwrite control variables.

If you want to do the reverse of this function (convert a series of variables into an array), use the **compact** function; just be aware that you only use the variable name and not the preceding $ character in the compact function. Here is some sample code:

```
$Drums = "John Mayhew" ;
$LeadGuitar = "Anthony Phillips" ;

$Genesis = array("Keyboards" => "Tony Banks", "Drums" => "Phil Collins",
```

```
    "BassGuitar" =>"Mike Rutherford","LeadGuitar" => "Steve Hackett",
    "Vocals" =>"Peter Gabriel" ) ;

    extract ($Genesis, EXTR_SKIP);
    echo "Original Genesis Lineup: $Keyboards, $Drums, $BassGuitar,
    $LeadGuitar, $Vocals" ;

    extract ($Genesis);
    echo "<br/>Classic Genesis Lineup: $Keyboards, $Drums, $BassGuitar,
    $LeadGuitar, $Vocals" ;

    $newGenesis = compact(Keyboards, Drums, BassGuitar, LeadGuitar, Vocals) ;
    echo "<br/>";
    var_dump($newGenesis);
```

Notice that the first extract example uses the optional parameter EXTR_SKIP. This is a directive to the function telling it to skip any variables that already exist. As shown in the output, the $Drums and $LeadGuitar variables are left as is:

Original Genesis Lineup: Tony Banks, John Mayhew, Mike Rutherford, Anthony Phillips, Peter Gabriel
Classic Genesis Lineup: Tony Banks, Phil Collins, Mike Rutherford, Steve Hackett, Peter Gabriel
array(5) { ["Keyboards"]=> string(10) "Tony Banks" ["Drums"]=> string(12) "Phil Collins" ["BassGuitar"]=> string(15) "Mike Rutherford" ["LeadGuitar"]=> string(13) "Steve Hackett" ["Vocals"]=> string(13) "Peter Gabriel" }

 There are a number of different directive options that you can use here, so be sure to look those up at *http://www.php.net/extract*.

If you want to combine two or more arrays together into one larger array, use the array_merge function. This will perform as advertised and simply concatenate two or more arrays into one without concern for duplicate values.

 If you are merging arrays with associative keys that are the same, the last key being brought into the merge will overwrite the previous one. If you are combining indexed arrays with similarly numbered numeric keys, the numbers will be reordered if there is a conflict.

Here is some sample code, followed by its output:

```
    $test1grades = array(1 => 87, 2 => 88,98,74,56,94,67,98,49) ;
    $test2grades = array(1 => 67, 2 => 76,78,98,56,93,68,95,83) ;

    $allgrades = array_merge($test1grades, $test2grades);
    var_dump($allgrades);
    echo "<br/><br/>";
```

```php
$Genesis1 = array("Keyboards" => "Tony Banks", "Drums" => "Phil Collins",
"BassGuitar" =>"Mike Rutherford","LeadGuitar" => "Steve Hackett",
"Vocals" =>"Peter Gabriel" ) ;

$Genesis2 = array("Keyboards" => "Tony Banks",
"Concert Drums" => "Chester Thompson",
"BassGuitar" =>"Mike Rutherford","LeadGuitar" => "Mike Rutherford",
"ConcertLeadGuitar" => "Daryl Sturmer", "Vocals" =>"Phil Collins" ) ;

$allGenesis = array_merge($Genesis1, $Genesis2);
var_dump($allGenesis);
```

array(18) { [0]=> int(87) [1]=> int(88) [2]=> int(98) [3]=> int(74) [4]=> int(56) [5]=> int(94) [6]=> int(67) [7]=> int(98) [8]=> int(49) [9]=> int(67) [10]=> int(76) [11]=> int(78) [12]=> int(98) [13]=> int(56) [14]=> int(93) [15]=> int(68) [16]=> int(95) [17]=> int(83) }

array(7) { ["Keyboards"]=> string(10) "Tony Banks" ["Drums"]=> string(12) "Phil Collins" ["BassGuitar"]=> string(15) "Mike Rutherford" ["LeadGuitar"]=> string(15) "Mike Rutherford" ["Vocals"]=> string(12) "Phil Collins" ["Concert Drums"]=> string(16) "Chester Thompson" ["ConcertLeadGuitar"]=> string(13) "Daryl Sturmer" }

The last good function we should look at in the context of arrays is array_walk. This function does double duty in that it calls a named function and passes each element to the called function as it steps through each element of an array. You can think of it as a more concise foreach loop on an array. In the following sample code, we'll call a function and have it add 10 to each grade in the array, then echo those new values to the browser. This function takes the value of the array first and, optionally, can also send the key.

```php
function add10($value ) {
    $value += 10 ;
    echo $value . " " ;
}

$testgrades = array(87,88,98,74,56,94,67,98,49) ;
var_dump($testgrades);
echo "<br/><br/>";
array_walk($testgrades, 'add10');
```

array(9) { [0]=> int(87) [1]=> int(88) [2]=> int(98) [3]=> int(74) [4]=> int(56) [5]=> int(94) [6]=> int(67) [7]=> int(98) [8]=> int(49) }

97 98 108 84 66 104 77 108 59

There are many more array functions that we did not look at in this chapter, so be sure to check them out on php.net (*http://php.net/index.php*), and don't be afraid to experiment with them to see what they can do for you!

CHAPTER 6

Objects

In this chapter we will look at object-oriented programming (OOP) and focus on the best parts of it as embodied in PHP. OOP has been around for many years and is certainly a very mature programming approach in the IT world. However, it is just recently (in the last five to seven years), coming into prominence in the web side of programming. This is a good thing, too, as it makes web programming that much more robust.

Classes, objects, polymorphism, encapsulation, inheritance, methods, and properties—these are buzz words of OOP that are usually thrown around without much care. Let's look at the definitions of these terms and then look at a sample collection of classes and see how they can work in concert.

Classes
> Classes are the definition or template of the code that is to be activated in an object. You will see and edit this code, but when it is executed it will run as an object. The class is copied into existence each time it is used in your code.

Objects
> An object is the copied and active form of a class. You may have heard of the term *instantiation*—this is just a big word for making a copy of an object in memory and giving it a unique name. When instantiating a class into an object in PHP, the new keyword is required.

Methods
> A method is merely a function written within the confines of a class. In PHP, we use the word *function* to refer to class writing instead of *method*.

Properties
> Properties are variables that also reside within the confines of a class.

Polymorphism
> This is another big word, and it really means that OOP allows for two separate classes to have the same content names, like methods and properties, without getting in each other's way. So, you can have two classes, each with a print method,

for example, and PHP will not be confused, mainly because PHP requires that object names be unique.

Encapsulation

Encapsulation is another feature of OOP that PHP makes use of. Encapsulation allows you to protect the data (properties) of a class from outside influences by using specific methods that exist within the class for the sole purpose of managing internal class properties. This is further explained in the section "Public, Protected, and Private" on page 68.

Inheritance

This OOP feature allows you to copy or inherit from what is known as a *super-class* (or *parent class*). If you have one class called "person" with some methods and properties defined, and you want to create another class that is a type of person, say "lumberjack," you can use all the attributes of the person class, like name, height, eye color, and so on, and extend that data into the lumberjack class, thus saving time and effort.

Putting It into Practice

Now let's look at some code that will help to explain most of the above concepts. First, let me set the groundwork for the classes that we will be using and how we will use them. I have kept this discussion from being overly complex, in hopes that you will be able to grasp the basics of OOP and see just how much you can accomplish with this programming approach.

 If you are already familiar with OOP from another language, you can skip ahead to the next section. Every language has its own nuances in how it implements OOP, so if something seems a little off, be sure to check back here for some clarity.

To begin, let's look at the classes we can use to build a basic web page with a data entry form on it. The data entry form will be very simple in that it will only ask for a first name, a last name, and a comment (similar to a guestbook form). One class will define methods for building basic HTML tags and one class will handle the parts of the form. We will use yet another class to build HTML table tags, since that HTML category is a little more specialized. We won't do the class code for every HTML tag, just the ones that we will use for this one page example. However, you can use the code shown here to develop any other HTML tag you want.

There is a lot of code here, so take some time to read through it and try to identify the parts that were defined earlier in this chapter.

Here is the code to build the html class:

```php
class html {

    // class properties (variables) are defined first
    private $tag ;

    // next define the methods (class functions)

    function __construct ($title="") {
        // class constructor, this builds the top of the HTML page
        // each time the class is constructed
        $this->tag = "<HTML> " ;
        $this->tag .= "<HEAD>" ;
        $this->tag .= "<title> $title </title>" ;
        $this->tag .= "</HEAD><BODY>" ;
        echo $this->tag ;
        return ;
    }

    function page_end () {
        // end of the HTML page, close the body
        // and the html tags
        $this->tag = "</BODY></HTML>" ;
        return $this->tag ;
    }

    function RawText($textString, $textColor="black", $bgcolor='', $fontSize="",
        $fontWeight="normal") {
        // this method is for sending raw unformatted text to the browser
        $this->tag = "<span style='color: $textColor ; background-color: $bgcolor ;
        font-size: $fontSize ; font-weight: $fontWeight'>" ;
        $this->tag .=  "$textString";
        $this->tag .=  "</span>" ;
        return $this->tag ;
    }

    function Image($source, $title="", $height="", $width="", $align="center",
        $border=0, $valign="middle",
    $class="", $id="", $name="", $onType1="", $onAction1="",
        $onType2="", $onAction2="", $onType3="", $onAction3="") {
        // this method is for adding images to the html page, it has
        // room for up to 3 onactions (onclick, onblur, onmouseup, etc)for
            each method call
        $this->tag = '<img src="' . $source . '" ' ;
        if ($name) $this->tag .= 'name="' . $name . '" ' ;
        if ($height == "") $height = "16" ;
        if ($width == "") $width = "16" ;
        $this->tag .= 'height="' . $height . '" width="' . $width . '" ' ;
        $this->tag .= 'border="' . $border . '" ' ;
        if ($class)     $this->tag .= 'class="' . $class . '" ' ;
        if ($id)      $this->tag .= 'id="' . $id . '" ' ;
        if ($title)     $this->tag .= 'title="' . $title . '" alt="' .
                        $title . '" ' ;
        if ($align)     $this->tag .= 'align="' . $align . '" ' ;
        if ($valign)    $this->tag .= 'valign="' . $valign . '" ' ;
        if ($onType1)    $this->tag .= $onType1 . '="' . $onAction1 . '" ' ;
```

```
        if ($onType2)      $this->tag .= $onType2 . '="' . $onAction2 . '" ' ;
        if ($onType3)      $this->tag .= $onType3 . '="' . $onAction3 . '" ' ;
        $this->tag .= "/>" ;
        return $this->tag ;
    }

    function Spacer($spaces = 1) {
        $this->tag = "";
        for ($i=1 ; $i <= $spaces ; $i++) {
            $this->tag .= " " ;
        }
        return $this->tag;
    }

    function NewLine($number = 1) {
        $this->tag = '';
        for ($i=1 ; $i <= $number ; $i++) {
            $this->tag .= "<br/>" ;
        }
        return $this->tag;
    }

} //end class: html
```

Here is the code to build the `table` class:

```
class table {

    private $tag ;

    function Begin($border=0, $align="center", $width='100%', $cellpadding=2,
        $cellspacing=2, $class='', $id='', $bgcolor='', $style='') {
        $this->tag = '<table ' ;
        if ($align)             $this->tag .= 'align="' . $align . '" ' ;
        if ($width)             $this->tag .= 'width="' . $width . '" ' ;
        if ($border > 0)        $this->tag .= 'border="' . $border . '" ' ;
        if ($cellpadding > 0)   $this->tag .= 'cellpadding="' . $cellpadding . '" ' ;
        if ($cellspacing > 0)   $this->tag .= 'cellspacing="' . $cellspacing . '" ' ;
        if ($class)             $this->tag .= 'class="' . $class . '" ' ;
        if ($id)                $this->tag .= 'id="' . $id . '" ' ;
        if ($bgcolor)             $this->tag .= 'bgcolor="' . $bgcolor . '" ' ;
        if ($style)             $this->tag .= 'style="' . $style . '" ' ;
        $this->tag .= ">" ;
        return $this->tag ;
    }

    function Header($text) {
        $this->tag = '<th>' . $text . '</th>' ;
        return $this->tag ;
    }

    function RowOn($align="", $bgcolor="", $class="", $height="") {
        $this->tag = '<tr ' ;
        if ($align)     $this->tag .= 'align="' . $align . '" ' ;
        if ($bgcolor)   $this->tag .= 'bgcolor="' . $bgcolor . '" ' ;
        if ($class)     $this->tag .= 'class="' . $class . '" ' ;
```

```
            if ($height)      $this->tag .= 'height="' . $height . '" ' ;
            $this->tag .= ">" ;
            return $this->tag ;
        }

        function ColumnOn($colspan=1, $align='left',  $width="", $rowspan="",
            $bgcolor="", $class="", $valign="", $height="") {
            $this->tag = '<td ' ;
            if ($align)      $this->tag .= 'align="' . $align . '" ' ;
            if ($colspan)     $this->tag .= 'colspan="' . $colspan . '" ' ;
            if ($width)      $this->tag .= 'width="' . $width . '" ' ;
            if ($rowspan)     $this->tag .= 'rowspan="' . $rowspan . '" ' ;
            if ($bgcolor)     $this->tag .= 'bgcolor="' . $bgcolor . '" ' ;
            if ($class)      $this->tag .= 'class="' . $class . '" ' ;
            if ($height)      $this->tag .= 'height"' . $height . '" ';
            if ($valign)      $this->tag .= "valign='" . $valign . "'>" ;
            if (!$valign)     $this->tag .= "valign='middle'>" ;
            return $this->tag ;
        }

        function ColumnOff() {
            $this->tag = '</td>' ;
            return $this->tag ;
        }

        function RowOff() {
            $this->tag = '</tr>' ;
            return $this->tag ;
        }

        function End() {
            $this->tag = '</table>' ;
            return $this->tag ;
        }
    } // end class table
```

Here is the code to build the **form** class:

```
class form {

    private $tag ;

    function Begin($action, $method='post', $name='', $id='', $style='', $class='') {
        $this->tag = '<form ' ;
        if ($method)     $this->tag .= 'method="' . $method . '" ' ;
        if ($action)     $this->tag .= 'action="' . $action . '" ' ;
        if ($name)       $this->tag .= 'name="' . $name . '" ' ;
        if ($id)         $this->tag .= 'id="' . $id . '" ' ;
        if ($style)      $this->tag .= 'style="' . $style . '" ' ;
        if ($class)      $this->tag .= 'class="' . $class . '" ' ;
        $this->tag .= "><input type='hidden' name='posted' value='1'>" ;
        return $this->tag ;
    }

    function HiddenValue($name, $value="") {
        $this->tag = '<input type="' . 'hidden' . '" ' ;
```

```php
            if ($name)     $this->tag .= 'name="' . $name . '" ' ;
            if ($value) $this->tag .= 'value="' . $value . '" ' ;
            $this->tag .= ">" ;
            return $this->tag ;
    }

    function InputLabel($textLabel, $labelFor, $required=false, $class='') {
            if ($required == true) $required = "<font color='red'>*</font>";
            $this->tag = '<label for="' . $labelFor . '" class="' . $class . '">' ;
            $this->tag .= $textLabel . $required;
            $this->tag .= ": </label>" ;
            return $this->tag ;
    }

    function Input($InputType, $EntityName, $value="", $align="center", $size="",
        $id="", $align="center", $readonly="", $class="",
        $onType1="", $onAction1="", $onType2="", $onAction2="",
        $onType3="", $onAction3="") {

            $this->tag = '<input type="' . $InputType . '" name="' . $EntityName
            . '" size="' . $size . '" ' ;
            if ($align)     $this->tag .= 'align="' . $align . '" ' ;
            if ($id)        $this->tag .= 'id="' . $id . '" ' ;
            if ($value == "on"){
                    $this->tag .= ' checked ';
                } elseif ($value){
                    $this->tag .= 'value="' . $value . '" ' ;
                }
            if ($class)     $this->tag .= 'class="' . $class . '" ' ;
            if ($onType1)       $this->tag .= $onType1 . '="' . $onAction1 . '" ' ;
            if ($onType2)       $this->tag .= $onType2 . '="' . $onAction2 . '" ' ;
            if ($onType3)       $this->tag .= $onType3 . '="' . $onAction3 . '" ' ;
            if ($readonly)      $this->tag .= 'readonly ' ;
            $this->tag .= ">" ;
            return $this->tag ;
    }

    function Textarea($name, $cols, $rows, $value="", $align="left", $class="",
        $readonly="", $onType1="", $onAction1="", $onType2="", $onAction2="",
        $onType3="", $onAction3="") {
            $this->tag = '<textarea name="' . $name . '" cols="'
            . $cols . '" rows="' . $rows . '" ' ;
            if ($align)     $this->tag .= 'align="' . $align . '" ' ;
            if ($class)     $this->tag .= 'class="' . $class . '" ' ;
            if ($onType1)       $this->tag .= $onType1 . '="' . $onAction1 . '" ' ;
            if ($onType2)       $this->tag .= $onType2 . '="' . $onAction2 . '" ' ;
            if ($onType3)       $this->tag .= $onType3 . '="' . $onAction3 . '" ' ;
            if ($readonly)      $this->tag .= 'readonly ' ;
            $this->tag .= ">$value</textarea>" ;
            return $this->tag ;
    }

function form_end(){
        return '</form>' ;
```

```
    }
  } // end class form
```

It makes great sense to save these files as separate includable files; I would save them as *html_class.inc*, *table_class.inc*, and *form_class.inc*, respectively, and then include them—or better still, require them—into the code file where they will be used. These three files are just the object definitions (the classes) and it does look like a lot of code for little gain (or, as they say in my part of the world, trying to drive in a thumbtack with a sledgehammer).

In PHP, if you want to create (instantiate) an active class (an object) use the new keyword. Here is an example of the top part of a file that is using and instantiating all three classes:

```
// require classes for the page
require_once ('classes/html_class.inc');
require_once ('classes/table_class.inc');
require_once ('classes/form_class.inc');

// instantiate classes (prepare them for use)
$HTMLPage    = new html("GuestBook Page") ;
$MyTable     = new table() ;
$MyForm      = new form() ;
```

Next, we want to start using the methods within these classes to build a web page that will accept a first name with a display of 30 characters, a last name with a display of 40 characters, and a comment area of 8 rows and 40 columns. Again, we will keep it simple in design and process, just to get the points of OPP across. Hopefully, you will be able to extrapolate this context into a fully operational OOP library.

So let's get back to the design of the web page form. Figure 6-1 shows the simple form for which we will be writing the code below.

Magic Methods

You may notice that in the HTML class definition there is a function called __construct. This is a special method that you can define for each class that is triggered (executed) each time the class is instantiated. What we are doing here is establishing the basic top of an HTML page at the same time that we are creating the object in memory. Additionally, we are passing in a value that will be used for the page title. This __construct method is actually looked for and executed each time a class is instantiated, whether or not the code for the method is actually written. If the method is not written, it will be called, but nothing will happen visibly.

The automatic method we use here (__construct) is part of a collection of predefined methods known as *magic methods*. These magic methods are all inherently defined within each class that you build within PHP. Even if you don't write the code for them yourself, they still exist and the PHP parser will use them or call them as needed,

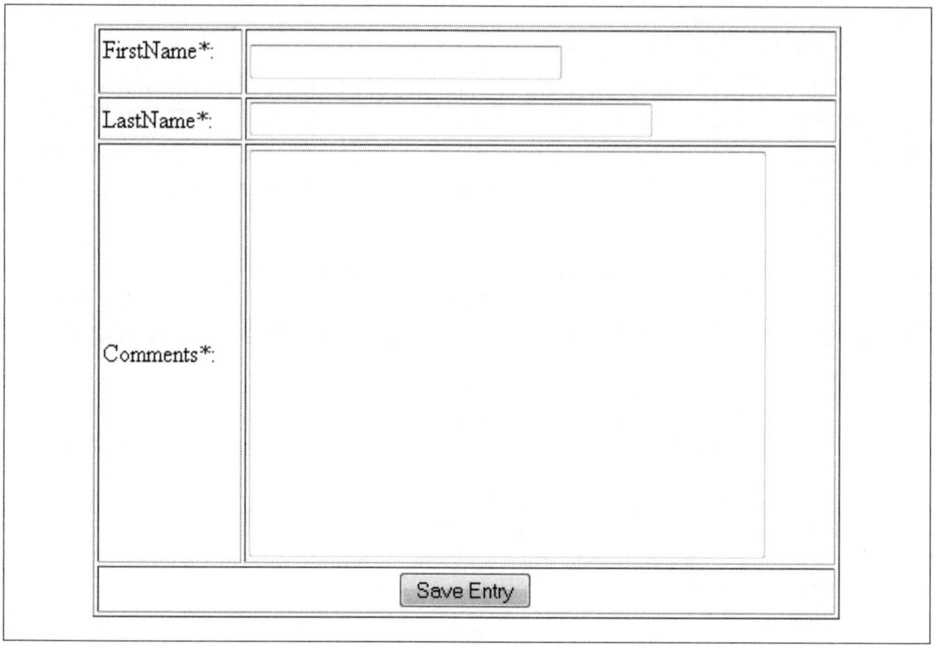

FirstName*:	
LastName*:	
Comments*:	
Save Entry	

Figure 6-1. A simple form generated by object-oriented code

although the definition will be that of the default behaviour PHP has assigned to it. Another magic method that is quite often used is the destructor method (__destruct). It is called when an object is removed from active use or when a script ends. If you want something special to be performed as the object is being destroyed, create this method within your class definition and add your desired code to it.

 You may notice in the HTML class code that there is a __construct method echoing out the content of the top of a web page (<HTML><HEAD>, etc.). This is merely an example of the use of one of the magic methods. Also note that this method is not returning a value, as magic methods are not permitted to do so.

Be sure to look up the other magic methods on the PHP website (*http://www.php.net/manual/en/language.oop5.magic.php*).

$this

In the class code above, you can see a variable called $this. $this is an internal and reserved variable used within the defined objects. You don't have to predefine it; it will be there for your use as soon as a class in instantiated into an object. It is used for internal references to properties, as can be seen in its referential use in relation to the

`$this->tag` variable. In fact, you have to use the `$this->` prefix to make internal reference to a class property.

Objects in Action

Here is the code creating the remainder of the page. We will briefly dissect it following the listing:

```
// start a table with a border, left alignment, and 30% width
$webpage = $MyTable->Begin(1, "left", "500") ;
$webpage .= $MyTable->RowOn();
$webpage .= $MyTable->ColumnOn();
$webpage .= $MyForm->Begin() ; // "proof" of polymorphism
$webpage .= $MyForm->InputLabel("FirstName","fname", true);
$webpage .= $MyTable->ColumnOff();
$webpage .= $MyTable->ColumnOn(1,"left");
$webpage .= $MyForm->Input("text", "fname", "", "", 30);
$webpage .= $MyTable->ColumnOff();
$webpage .= $MyTable->RowOff();

$webpage .= $MyTable->RowOn();
$webpage .= $MyTable->ColumnOn();
$webpage .= $MyForm->InputLabel("LastName","lname", true);
$webpage .= $MyTable->ColumnOff();
$webpage .= $MyTable->ColumnOn();
$webpage .= $MyForm->Input("text", "lname", "", "", 40);
$webpage .= $MyTable->ColumnOff();
$webpage .= $MyTable->RowOff();

$webpage .= $MyTable->RowOn();
$webpage .= $MyTable->ColumnOn();
$webpage .= $MyForm->InputLabel("Comments","comments", true);
$webpage .= $MyTable->ColumnOff();
$webpage .= $MyTable->ColumnOn();
$webpage .= $MyForm->Textarea("comments", 40, 15);
$webpage .= $MyTable->ColumnOff();
$webpage .= $MyTable->RowOff();

$webpage .= $MyTable->RowOn();
$webpage .= $MyTable->ColumnOn(2, "center");
$webpage .= $MyForm->Input("submit", "submit", "Save Entry");
$webpage .= $MyTable->ColumnOff();
$webpage .= $MyTable->RowOff();

$webpage .= $MyForm->form_end();
$webpage .= $MyTable->End();

$webpage .= $HTMLPage->page_end() ;

echo $webpage ;
```

As you can see, the code uses an output variable called **$webpage** to store all the returned values from the class methods that are called to construct this page. On each page, there are functions (methods) of the class that you cannot use. In the `html` class, for example, only the constructor and the `page_end` methods are used. This is normal behavior—you don't always use every screwdriver in your toolbox for each odd-job task.

Notice that many of the method calls do not pass their defined parameters. This is a feature of PHP that also affects user-defined functions: you can set default values on a method's definitions and use those defaults if nothing is passed for that particular parameter. Look at this line of code:

```
$webpage .= $MyForm->Begin("save_entry.php") ;
```

There is only one parameter passed to the method, while the class definition looks like this:

```
function Begin($action, $method='post', $name='', $id='', $style='', $class='')
```

The parameters all have preset default values except for the first one (`$action`). Some of these parameters are empty and therefore generally unused. Actually, you don't even have to list these optional parameters in the method call if you don't want to; they are optional in the sense that they have preset values. In this case, you must provide the `$action` parameter, because it does not have a preset value. It is always good practice to have the required elements at the beginning of the parameter list. In fact, PHP won't work very well (if at all) if the required elements are not at the front of the list. If you find your parameter lists getting too long, consider using an array or two to send them over. When looking at the generated HTML `<form>` tag in the web page's HTML, it looks like this: `<form method="post" action="save_entry.php" >`, so, at the very least, we will always have the required action parameter and a POST method on our `<form>` tags.

Public, Protected, and Private

Just as you can set scope in procedural PHP, you can also set it in the OOP aspect of PHP. You can identify your properties and your methods as either *public*, *protected*, or *private*. An entity with public scope is open to use and access outside the class definition itself. An entity with protected scope is only accessible within the class in which it is defined and its parent or inherited classes. Finally, an entity with private scope is only accessible within the class that defines it.

Encapsulation, the concept of protecting entities within a class from any outside influences, can best be achieved using the `private` scope attribute. A little later in this chapter, we will look at a `person` class to see this in action. Basically, it is always best to limit the scope access of a class from outside influences, especially if you are writing a class library that will be used in many different projects or if you are making a commercially available library. This protects your code from being tripped up in any way, either by improper use or by directly accessing its properties from outside the class itself. The protected scope is rarely used unless you have a heredity tree (inherited classes) that can benefit in some way. The public scope is the default scope if none is declared, and it is used best on methods that allow the class to interface with the outside world. The best way to share information to an outside entity that is making use of your class is with the public get and set methods (a.k.a. accessor methods) that act on the privately declared class properties. We'll look at this more closely in the following section.

Getters and Setters

The last major portions of the OOP model that we'll look at in this chapter are the get and set methods for the class properties. This concept allows for a more protected interface within the class itself. Each class property has its own get and set methods, and the only way to affect each property is through the use of these accessor methods. Here is a person class that has the properties firstname, lastname, and gender, with get and set methods for all three properties:

```php
class person {

    private $firstname ;
    private $lastname ;
    private $gender ;

    public function getFirstname() {
        return $this->firstname;
    }

    public function getLastname() {
        return $this->lastname;
    }

    public function getGender() {
        return $this->gender;
    }

    public function setFirstname($firstname) {
        $this->firstname = $firstname;
    }

    public function setLastname($lastname) {
        $this->lastname = $lastname;
    }

    public function setGender($gender) {
        $this->gender = $gender;
    }

} //end class: person
```

You may add validation code to the set methods if you wish. This allows for more accurate data being handled through the class itself before the value is actually set. For example, in the setGender method above, you can verify that it is the male/female (M/F) data you are looking for (rejecting any invalid entries like K or Q) before you accept the value.

Notice that there is no constructor method here; this is perfectly fine, as PHP will look for the _construct method and run it if it is found, and will do nothing except create the class in memory if the method is not found. To call this class into existence and make use of the accessor methods, you can do something like this:

```
$newPerson = new person() ;
$newPerson->setFirstname("Peter") ;
$newPerson->setLastname("MacIntyre") ;
$newPerson->setGender("male");

echo "the Person class currently has these values: " ;
echo "<br/> First Name:" . $newPerson->getFirstname() ;
echo "<br/> Last Name: " . $newPerson->getLastname() ;
echo "<br/> Gender: " . $newPerson->getGender() ;
```

The above code will produce the following output:

```
the Person class currently has these values:
First Name:Peter
Last Name: MacIntyre
Gender: male
```

As you can see here, there is no direct call to any of the three properties of this class. For example, we cannot write the following:

```
echo $newPerson->lastname ;
```

There are many other aspects of OOP PHP that we have not touched on here—topics like inheritance, interfaces, object cloning, late static binding, and so on. My purpose in this chapter was simply to demonstrate the power and simplicity of the OOP approach to web programming, and to give a concise example of it in practical use. For a full and thorough explanation of OOP in PHP, I recommend the book *Object Oriented PHP* (No Starch Press) by Peter Lavin.

CHAPTER 7

Database Interaction

It would make little sense these days to have a static website that doesn't change unless you physically alter the HTML or PHP of each file. There is usually a need to store and retrieve dynamic information as it relates to the content of a website or web application. In this chapter, we will look at how to make your pages draw some of their content from a database.

MySQLi Object Interface

The most popular database platform used with PHP is the MySQL database. If you look at the MySQL website (*http://www.mysql.com/*) you will discover that there are a few different versions of MySQL you can use. We will look at the freely distributable version known as the *community server*. PHP has a number of different interfaces to this database tool as well, so we will look at the object-oriented interface known as MySQL Improved extension (MySQLi). If you read the previous chapter on OOP with PHP, the use of this interface should not be overly foreign.

First, let's use the very basic database schema I hinted at in the previous chapter by extending the example of a rudimentary guestbook page we started with. We'll add the ability to actually save the entries into the database table. Here is the structure of the *guests* table:

```
table: guests
guestid  int(11)
fname       varchar(30)
lname       varchar(40)
comments text
```

And here is the SQL code to create it:

```
CREATE DATABASE 'website' ;
USE 'website' ;

CREATE TABLE 'guests' (
'guestid' INT NOT NULL AUTO_INCREMENT PRIMARY KEY ,
'fname' VARCHAR( 30 ) NOT NULL ,
```

```
'lname' VARCHAR( 40 ) NOT NULL ,
'comments' TEXT NOT NULL
)
```

Since this object-oriented interface is built into PHP with a standard installation configuration (you just have to activate the MySQL extension in your PHP environment), all you have to do to start using it is instantiate its class, as in the following code:

```
$mydb = new mysqli('localhost', 'dbuser', 'dbpassword', 'dbname');
```

In our example, we have a database named website, and we will pretend that our username is petermac with the password 1q2w3e4r. The actual code that we use is:

```
$mydb = new mysqli('localhost', 'petermac', '1q2w3e4r', 'website');
```

This gives us access to the database engine itself within the PHP code; we will specifically access tables and other data later. Once this class is instantiated into the variable $mydb, we can use methods on that object to do our database work.

 This chapter assumes an understanding of the SQL command language and will not spend time covering it. There are many online resources and printed books that can assist you with crafting SQL code.

We will now write the additional code that is required for our example in order to store the information into the *guests* table. We have to update the $webpage .= $MyForm->Begin() ; line of code to send the action parameter to the object so that we can process the submitted form. Our destination file is called *save_data.php*, so the line of code will now be:

```
$webpage .= $MyForm->Begin('save_data.php') ;
```

This file will take the values from the $_POST array and save them into the database. Here is the full listing of the code:

```
$mydb = new mysqli('localhost', 'petermac', '1q2w3e4r', 'website');

$sql = "INSERT INTO guests (fname, lname, comments)
VALUES ('$_POST[fname]', '$_POST[lname]', '$_POST[comments]')";

if ($mydb->query($sql)  == TRUE) {
    echo "Guest entry saved successfully.";
} else {
    echo "INSERT attempt failed, please try again later, or call tech support" ;
}

$mydb->close();
```

For the sake of simplicity and clarity, we are not concerned here with security of the content coming from the user (`$_POST` array). Be sure to review Chapter 9 on security, particularly the section titled "Cross-Site Scripting (XXS) and SQL Injection" on page 115 before you use any of your SQL code on a public site.

First, we instantiate the `MySQLi` class into an object with the variable identifier `$mydb`. Next, we build our SQL command string and save it to a variable called `$sql`. Then we call the query method of the class, and at the same time test its return value to determine if it was successful (true) and comment to the screen accordingly. Last, we call the `close` method on the class to tidy up and destroy the class from memory.

Retrieving Data for Display

In another area of your website, you may want to draw out a listing of your guests and show a short clip of their comments. We can accomplish this by employing the same `MySQLi` class and working with the result set that is generated from a SELECT SQL command. There are many ways to display the information in the browser, and we'll look at one example of how this can be done. Notice that the returned result is a different object than the `$mydb` that we first instantiate. PHP instantiates the result object for you and fills it with any returned data. Here is the code:

```
$mydb = new mysqli('localhost', 'petermac', '1q2w3e4r', 'website');

$sql = "SELECT * FROM Guests ORDER BY lname, fname";

$result = $mydb->query($sql);

while( $row = $result->fetch_assoc() ){
    echo $row['fname'] . " " . $row['lname'] ;
    echo " made these comments: " . substr($row['comments'],0,150) ;
    echo "<br/>";
}

$result->close();

$mydb->close ();
```

Here, we are using the `query` method call and storing the returned information into the variable called `$result`. Then, we use a method of the result object called `fetch_assoc` to provide one row of data at a time, and we store that single row into the variable called `$row`. This continues while there are rows to process, and within that `while` loop, we are dumping content out to the browser window. Finally, we close both the result and the database objects.

One of the most useful methods I have found in MySQLi is `multi_query`; this method allows you to run multiple SQL commands in the same statement. If you want to do an INSERT, and then an UPDATE statement based on similar data, you can do it all in one method call.

We have, of course, just scratched the surface of what the `MySQLi` class has to offer. You can find the documentation for the class at *http://www.php.net/mysqli*, and you will see the extensive list of methods that are part of this class. Each result class is documented within the appropriate subject area.

PHP Data Objects

Next, we will look at PHP Data Objects (PDO). This is another interface to the database world that is provided within PHP. The major difference between PDO and MySQLi is that the `MySQLi` class is limited to interfacing with a MySQL database engine, whereas PDO has additional drivers for many database platforms and you can use the same PDO methods on any supported database engine; just be sure your underlying SQL syntax still works on the new database engine. Here is a list of the available platforms at the time of this writing:

- Microsoft SQL Server and Sybase
- Firebird/Interbase
- IBM
- Informix
- MySQL
- Oracle
- ODBC and DB2
- PostgreSQL
- SQLite
- Driver 4D for PDO

To use PDO, however, you have to direct PHP to use the desired interface. You can do this in the *php.ini* file, as shown here in a Windows environment enabling the MySQL extension:

```
extension=php_pdo.dll
extension=php_pdo_mysql.dll
```

If you want to switch to another database platform, Informix for example, merely disable the MySQL extension and insert the one for Informix:

```
extension=php_pdo.dll
//extension=php_pdo_mysql.dll
extension=php_pdo_informix.dll
```

You should now have all of your database code talking to the new database engine. Of course, you can also have multiple PDO engines running at the same time if you like. In that case, simply add the new directive and leave the first one intact.

If we repeat the two examples that we used earlier in this chapter with the PDO interface, the first piece of code will look like this:

```
$dsn = 'mysql:dbname=website;host=localhost';
$myPDO = new PDO($dsn, 'petermac', '1q2w3e4r');

$sql = "INSERT INTO guests (fname, lname, comments)
VALUES ('$_POST[fname]', '$_POST[lname]', '$_POST[comments]')";

$result = $myPDO->query($sql) ;

if ( $result !== False ) {
    echo "Guest entry saved successfully.";
} else {
    echo "INSERT attempt failed, please try again later, or call tech support" ;
}
```

This code clearly has a similar footprint to the code in our first example. However, there is a new line of code where the **$dsn** is defined—this is simply how the PDO object connects to its database engine. Actually, you must alter this one line of code if you choose to interface with another database platform (but if you put the first two lines of code into an included file, you only have to change one line of code throughout your web project).

Here, too, we are accepting the result of the executed query into a variable. Even though there are no rows of data returned on an insert statement, we can still verify that a result (empty) was returned (not false), therefore proving that the code ran correctly.

The second piece of code in PDO format would look like this:

```
$dsn = 'mysql:dbname=website;host=localhost';
$myPDO = new PDO($dsn, 'petermac', '1q2w3e4r');

$sql = "SELECT * FROM Guests ORDER BY lname, fname";

$result = $myPDO->query($sql);

while ($row = $result->fetch(PDO::FETCH_ASSOC)){
    echo $row['fname'] . " " . $row['lname'] ;
    echo " made these comments: " . substr($row['comments'],0,150) ;
    echo "<br/>";
}
```

PDO Prepared Statements

PDO lets you build what is called a *prepared statement* (MySQLi can also do this after a fashion). This is a process whereby you set up some SQL code that may be called repeatedly and only altered slightly. It will save you from recreating entire SQL command strings, and actually lends itself to writing more secure code. You can build these prepared statements with named placeholders or question mark placeholders; we will use examples of both in the following code. A named placeholder is a little more human-readable. Here is a variation of our SELECT sample code in which we will alter the ORDER BY clause:

```
$dsn = 'mysql:dbname=website;host=localhost';
$myPDO = new PDO($dsn, 'petermac', '1q2w3e4r');

$statement  = $myPDO->prepare('SELECT * FROM Guests ORDER BY ? ') ;
$statement->execute(array('lname'));

echo "List of Comments by Last Name <br/>";
while ($row = $statement->fetch(PDO::FETCH_ASSOC)){
    echo $row['fname'] . " " . $row['lname'] ;
    echo " made these comments: " . substr($row['comments'],0,150) ;
    echo "<br/>";
}

$statement->execute(array('fname'));

echo "List of Comments by First Name <br/>";
while ($row = $statement->fetch(PDO::FETCH_ASSOC)){
    echo $row['fname'] . " " . $row['lname'] ;
    echo " made these comments: " . substr($row['comments'],0,150) ;
    echo "<br/>";
}
```

Here we are repeating the use of the SQL statement and altering how the result is being sorted. All we have to do is recall the **execute** method with a different parameter, and the same SQL is run just slightly altered. This is an example of the question mark placeholder code, where the optional value is resolved by position. If there are more question mark placeholders, you need to ensure that the correct array is being passed into the statement on the **execute** method by confirming that everything is in the correct order. Here is the same code with named parameters instead; notice that it is in fact a little easier to read:

```
$statement  = $myPDO->prepare('SELECT * FROM Guests ORDER BY :ordervalue ') ;
$statement->execute(array('ordervalue' => 'lname'));

echo "List of Comments by Last Name <br/>";
while ($row = $statement->fetch(PDO::FETCH_ASSOC)){
    echo $row['fname'] . " " . $row['lname'] ;
    echo " made these comments: " . substr($row['comments'],0,150) ;
    echo "<br/>";
}

$statement->execute(array('ordervalue' => 'fname'));

echo "List of Comments by First Name <br/>";
while ($row = $statement->fetch(PDO::FETCH_ASSOC)){
    echo $row['fname'] . " " . $row['lname'] ;
    echo " made these comments: " . substr($row['comments'],0,150) ;
```

```
    echo "<br/>";
}
```

The named parameter in the SQL statement replaces the question mark, and the name is preceded with a colon (:) to identify it in the prepared statement as being the variable value. Additionally, the array being passed into the statement has the name of the parameter included as the key of the array value, also for clarity. Prepared statements can certainly save time when the need to reuse SQL commands arises, and you will find that it is more useful for INSERT and UPDATE statements than for SELECT statements.

 Both MySQLi and PDO can be transaction-based in their behavior with a database. This is of great value if you want to execute a number of SQL statements that all have to be successful (like a banking transaction) for any of the actions to be finalized in the database. Be sure to look into this feature if your web application requires this functionality.

If you are expecting input from an outside source, like a data entry form, be sure to consider the PDO quote method. In conjunction with basic security best practices (see Chapter 9), this quote method places quotes around the provided data and escapes any special characters within that provided data.

PDO, like MySQLi, has a lot to offer and you should certainly look into its use, especially if you expect to be developing an application that cannot be locked into a single database platform. To completely cover it here would mean discussing variations on a theme, and reworking these similar things is outside the scope of this slender volume. But do be aware of its availability.

Data Management on the Cheap

So far in this chapter we have looked at data management with a database engine interface. There are two other approaches that you should also consider when you are looking into data management: the use of the lightweight database interface called SQLite, and data management through file access. These options are rarely considered except for special cases like mobile technology (such as Android) and, to be fair, one can see how this would be the case when only a cursory glance is given to them. But let's take a closer look here.

SQLite

The SQLite database tool is available by default in PHP and has the same features as most of the other database tools. The catch here is that all the database storage is file-based, and is therefore accomplished without the use of a separate database engine. This can be very advantageous if you are trying to build an application with a small footprint and without depending on products other than PHP. Because SQLite is built into the standard deployment of PHP, all you have to do to start using it is to make reference to it.

 If you are using PHP 5.3, you may have to update your *php.ini* file to include this directive: `extension=php_sqlite.dll`, since at the time of this writing, the default directive (`extension=php_sqlite3.dll`) does not seem to have the same working content.

SQLite has an OOP interface, so you can instantiate an object with the following statement:

```
$database = new SQLiteDatabase('c:/copy/website.sqlite');
```

The neat thing about this statement is that if the file is not found at the specified location, SQLite will create it for you. Continuing with our *guests* database example, the command to create the table within SQLite would be like this:

```
$sql = 'CREATE TABLE guests (
guestid INTEGER PRIMARY KEY ,
fname TEXT ,
lname TEXT ,
comments TEXT )';

$database->queryExec($sql);
```

 In SQLite, unlike MySQL, there is no `AUTO_INCREMENT` option. SQLite instead makes any column that is defined with `INTEGER` and `PRIMARY KEY` an automatically incrementing column. You can override this by providing a value to the column when an `INSERT` statement is executed.

Notice here that the data types are quite different than what we have seen in MySQL. Remember that SQLite is a trimmed-down database tool and therefore it is "lite" on its data types; see Table 7-1 for a listing of the data types that SQLite uses.

Table 7-1. Data types available in SQLite

Data type	Explanation
Text	Stores data as NULL, TEXT, or BLOB content. If a number is supplied to a text field, it is converted to text before it is stored.
Numeric	Can store either integer or real data. If text data is supplied, an attempt is made to convert the information to numerical format.
Integer	Behaves the same as the numeric data type, however if data of real format is supplied, it is stored as an integer. This may affect data storage accuracy.
Real	Behaves the same as the numeric data type, except that it forces integer values into floating-point representation.
None	This is a catchall data type. This type does not prefer one base type to another. Data is stored exactly as supplied.

Run the following code just to get some data into the database file:

```
$sql =
  'INSERT INTO guests (fname, lname, comments) ' .
  'VALUES ("Peter", "MacIntyre", "Nice work pilgrim!"); ' .

  'INSERT INTO guests (fname, lname, comments) ' .
  'VALUES ("Dawn", "Riley", "Great site, love what you have
done with the place!"); ' .

  'INSERT INTO guests (fname, lname, comments) ' .
  'VALUES ("Peter", "MacIntyre", "Me again... just saying hello."); ' ;

$database->queryExec($sql) ;
```

Notice here that we can execute multiple SQL commands at the same time. This can also be done with MySQLi, but you have to remember to use the `multi_query` method there; with SQLite, it's available with the `queryExec` method. After loading the database with some data, run this code to produce some output:

```
$sql = "SELECT * FROM guests ORDER BY lname, fname";

$result = $database->query($sql);

while ($row = $result->fetch()){
    echo $row['fname'] . " " . $row['lname'] ;
    echo " made these comments: " . substr($row['comments'],0,150) ;
    echo "<br/>";
}
```

The above code produces the following output:

```
Peter MacIntyre made these comments: Me again... just saying hello.
Peter MacIntyre made these comments: Nice work pilgrim!
Dawn Riley made these comments: Great site, love what you have
done with the place!
```

SQLite has the capability to do almost as much as the "bigger" database engines, and the "lite" does not really mean light on functionality; rather, it is light on demand for system resources. You should always consider SQLite when you require a database that may need to be more portable and less demanding of resources.

 If you are just getting started with the dynamic aspect of web development, you can use PDO to interface with SQLite. In this way, you can start with a lightweight database and grow into a more robust database server like MySQL when you are ready.

File Management As a Database Alternative

PHP has many little hidden features within its vast toolset. One of these features (which is often overlooked) is its uncanny capability to handle complex files—sure, everyone knows that PHP can open a file, but what can it really do with that file? What actually brought the true range of possibilities to my attention was a request from a prospective client who had "no money," but wanted a dynamic web survey developed. Of course, I initially offered the client the wonders of PHP and database interaction with MySQLi. Upon hearing the monthly fees from a local ISP, however, the client asked if there was any other way to have the work accomplished. It turns out that if you don't want to use SQLite, another alternative is to use files to manage and manipulate small amounts of text for later retrieval. The functions we'll discuss here are nothing out of the ordinary when taken individually—in fact, they're really part of the basic PHP toolset everyone is probably familiar with, as you can see in Table 7-2.

Table 7-2. Commonly used PHP file management functions

Function name	Description of use
mkdir()	Used to make a directory on the server.
file_exists()	Used to determine if a file or directory exists at the supplied location.
fopen()	Used to open an existing file for reading or writing (see detailed options for correct usage).
fread()	Used to read in the contents of a file to a variable for PHP use.
flock()	Used to gain an exclusive lock on a file for writing.
fwrite()	Used to write the contents of a variable to a file.
filesize()	When reading in a file, this is used to determine how many bytes to read in at a time.
fclose()	Used to close the file once its usefulness has passed.

The interesting part is in tying all the functions together to accomplish your objective. For example, let's create a small web form survey that covers two pages of questions. The user can enter some opinions and return at a later date to finish the survey, picking up right where he left off. We'll scope out the logic of our little application and, hopefully, you will see that its basic premise can be expanded to full production-type employment.

The first thing that we want to do is allow the user to return to this survey at any time to provide additional input. To do this, we need to have a unique identifier to differentiate one user from another one. Generally, a person's email address is unique (other people might know it and use it, but that is a question of website security and/or controlling identity theft). For the sake of simplicity, we will assume honesty here in the use of email addresses and not bother with a password system. So, once we have the guest's email address, we need to store that information in a location that is distinct from that of other visitors. For this purpose, we will create a directory folder for each visitor on the server (this, of course, assumes that you have access and proper rights to a location on the server that permits the reading and writing of files). Because we have a relatively unique identifier in the visitor's email address, we will simply name the new directory location with that identifier. Once a directory is created (testing to see if the user has returned from a previous session), we will read in any file contents that are already there and display them in a <textarea> form control so that the visitor can see what (if anything) he has written previously. We then save his comments upon the submission of the form and move on to the next survey question. Here is the code for the first page (the `<?php` tags are included here because there are places where they are turned on and off throughout the listing):

```php
<?php
session_start();
if ($_POST['posted'] && $_POST['email'] != "") {

    $folder = "surveys/" . strtolower($_POST['email']);

    // send path information to the session
    $_SESSION['folder'] = $folder;

    if (!file_exists($folder)) {
        // make the directory and then add the empty files
        mkdir($folder);
    }

    header( "Location: page1.php" );

} else {  ?>
    <html>
    <head>
    <title>Files & folders - On-line Survey</title>
    </head>
    <body bgcolor="#FFFFFF" text="#000000">
    <h2>Survey Form </h2>
    <p>Please enter your e-mail address to start recording your comments</p>
    <form action="<?= $PHP_SELF ?>" method=POST>
    <input type="hidden" name="posted" value=1>
    <p>e-mail address: <input type="text" name="email" size="45" >
    <br/><br/>
    <input type="submit" name="submit" value="Submit">
    </form>

<?php } ?>

</body>
</html>
```

Figure 7-1 shows the web page that asks the visitor to submit his email address.

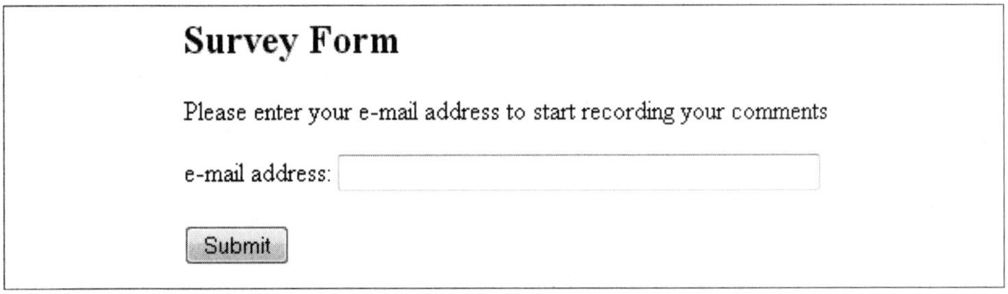

Figure 7-1. Survey login screen

As you can see, the first thing that we do is open a new session to pass the visitor's information on to subsequent pages. Then we perform a test to determine whether the form further down in the code has indeed been submitted and that there is something entered in the email address field. If this test fails, the form is simply redisplayed. Of course, the production version of this functionality would send out an error message telling the user to enter valid text.

Once this test has passed (assuming the form has been submitted correctly) we create a $folder variable that contains the directory structure where we want to save the survey information and append the user's email address to the end of it; we also save the contents of this newly created variable ($folder) into the session for later use. Here, we simply take the email address and use it (again, if this were a secure site, we would protect the data with proper security measures).

Next, we want to see if the directory already exists. If it does not, we create it with the mkdir() function. This function takes the argument of the path and the name of the directory we want to create and attempts to create it.

 In a Linux environment, there are other options on the mkdir() function that control access levels and permissions on the newly created directory, so be sure to look into those options if this applies to your environment.

After we verify that the directory exists, we simply direct the browser to the first page of the survey.

Now that we are on the first page of the survey (see Figure 7-2), the form is ready for the user to use.

Please enter your response to the following survey question:

What is your opinion on the state of the world economy? Can you help us fix it ?

[Submit]

Figure 7-2. The first page of the survey

This, however, is a dynamically generated form, as you can see in the following code:

```php
<?php
session_start();
$folder = $_SESSION['folder'];
$filename = $folder . "/question1.txt" ;

$file_handle = fopen($filename, "a+");
// open file for reading then clean it out
// pick up any text in the file that may already be there
$comments = fread($file_handle, filesize($filename));
fclose($file_handle); // close this handle

if ($_POST['posted']) {
    // create file if first time and then
    // save text that is in $_POST['question1']
    $question1 = $_POST['question1'];
    $file_handle = fopen($filename, "w+");
    // open file for total overwrite

    if (flock($file_handle, LOCK_EX)) {
        // do an exclusive lock
        if (fwrite($file_handle, $question1) == FALSE) {
            echo "Cannot write to file ($filename)";
        }
        flock($file_handle, LOCK_UN);
        // release the lock
    }

    // close the file handle and redirect to next page ?
    fclose($file_handle);
    header( "Location: page2.php" );

} else {

?>
    <html>
    <head>
    <title>Files & folders - On-line Survey</title>
    </head>
    <body>

    <table border=0><tr><td>
    Please enter your response to the following survey question:
    </td></tr>
    <tr bgcolor=lightblue><td>
    What is your opinion on the state of the world economy?<br/>
    Can you help us fix it ?
    </td></tr>
    <tr><td>
    <form action="<?= $PHP_SELF ?>" method=POST>
    <input type="hidden" name="posted" value=1>
    <br/>
    <textarea name="question1" rows=12 cols=35><?= $comments ?></textarea>
    </td></tr>
    <tr><td>
```

```
<input type="submit" name="submit" value="Submit">
</form></td></tr>
</table>
<?php } ?>
```

Let me highlight a few of the lines of code here, because this is where the file management and manipulation really takes place. After taking in the session information that we need and adding the filename to the end of the $filename variable, we are ready to start working with the files. Keep in mind that the point of this process is to display any information that may already be saved in the file and allow users to enter information (or alter what they have already entered). So, near the top of the code you see this command:

```
$file_handle = fopen($filename, "a+");
```

Using the file opening function, fopen(), we ask PHP to provide us with a handle to that file and store it in the variable suitably called $file_handle. Notice that there is another parameter passed to the function here: the a+ option. If you look at the PHP site (*http://php.net/index.php*), you will see a full listing of these option letters and what they mean. This one causes the file to open for reading and writing, with the file pointer placed at the end. If the file does not exist, PHP will attempt to create it. If you look at the next two lines of code, you will see that the entire file is read (using the file size() function to determine its size) into the $comments variable, and then it is closed.

```
$comments = fread($file_handle, filesize($filename));
fclose($file_handle);
```

Next, we want to see if the form portion of this program file has been executed, and, if so, we have to save any information that was entered into the text area. This time, we open the same file again, but we use the w+ option, which causes the interpreter to open the file for writing only—creating it if it doesn't exist, or emptying it if it does. The file pointer is placed at the beginning of the file. Essentially, we want to empty out the current contents of the file and replace it with a totally new volume of text. For this purpose, we employ the fwrite() function:

```
// do an exclusive lock
if (flock($file_handle, LOCK_EX)) {
    if (fwrite($file_handle, $question1) == FALSE){
        echo "Cannot write to file ($filename)";
    }
    // release the lock
    flock($file_handle, LOCK_UN);
}
```

We have to be sure that this information is indeed saved into the designated file, so we wrap a few conditional statements around our file writing operations to make sure everything will go smoothly. First, we attempt to gain an exclusive lock on the file in question (using the flock() function)—this will ensure no other process can access the file while we're operating on it. After the writing is complete, we release the lock on the file.

As you can see, the file write function uses `$file_handle` to add the contents of the `$question1` variable to the file. Then, we simply close the file when we are finished with it and move on to the next page of the survey, as shown in Figure 7-3.

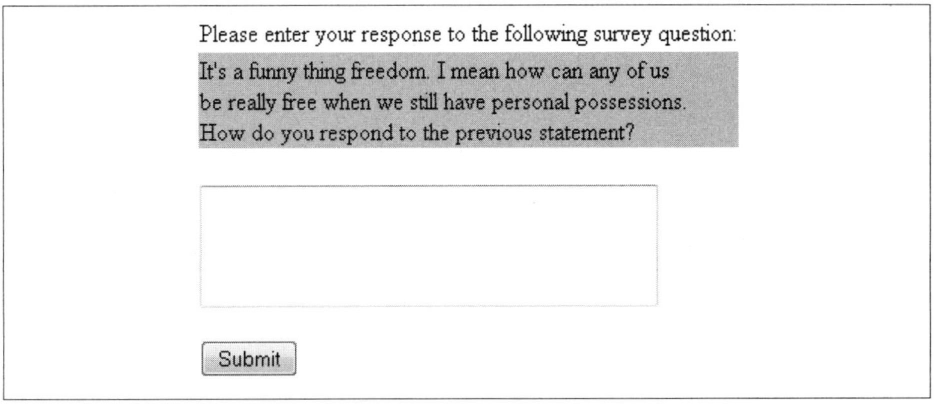

Please enter your response to the following survey question:

It's a funny thing freedom. I mean how can any of us be really free when we still have personal possessions. How do you respond to the previous statement?

Submit

Figure 7-3. Page 2 of the survey

As you can see in the following code for page 2 of the survey, the code for processing this next file (called *question2.txt*) is identical to the previous one, except for its name.

```php
<?php
session_start();
$folder = $_SESSION['folder'];
$filename = $folder . "/question2.txt" ;

$file_handle = fopen($filename, "a+");
// open file for reading then clean it out
// pick up any text in the file that may already be there
$comments = fread($file_handle, filesize($filename));
fclose($file_handle); // close this handle

if ($_POST['posted']) {
    // create file if first time and then save
    //text that is in $_POST['question1']
    $question2 = $_POST['question2'];
    $file_handle = fopen($filename, "w+");
    // open file for total overwrite

    if (flock($file_handle, LOCK_EX)) { // do an exclusive lock
        if (fwrite($file_handle, $question1) == FALSE) {
            echo "Cannot write to file ($filename)";
        }
        flock($file_handle, LOCK_UN); // release the lock
    }

    // close the file handle and redirect to next page ?
    fclose($file_handle);
    header( "Location: last_page.php" );
```

```
    } else {

?>
    <html>
    <head>
    <title>Files & folders - On-line Survey</title>
    </head>
    <body>

    <table border=0><tr><td>
    Please enter your comments to the following survey statement:
    </td></tr>
    <tr bgcolor=lightblue><td>
    It's a funny thing freedom. I mean how can any of us <br/>
    be really free when we still have personal possessions.
    How do you respond to the previous statement?
    </td></tr>
    <tr><td>
    <form action="<?= $PHP_SELF ?>" method=POST>
    <input type="hidden" name="posted" value=1>
    <br/>
    <textarea name="question2" rows=12 cols=35><?= $comments ?></textarea>
    </td></tr>
    <tr><td>
    <input type="submit" name="submit" value="Submit">
    </form></td></tr>
    </table>


    <?php } ?>
```

This kind of file processing can continue for as long as you like and, therefore, your surveys can be as long as you like. To make it more interesting, you can ask multiple questions on the same page and simply give each question its own filename.

Of course, after a few pages, with as many as five questions per page, you may find yourself with a large volume of individual files needing management. Fortunately, PHP has other file handling functions that you can use. The file() function, for example, is an alternative to the fread() function that reads the entire contents of a file in an array, one element per line. If your information is formatted properly—with each line delimited by the end of line sequence \n—you can store multiple pieces of information in a single file very easily. Naturally, this would also entail the use of the appropriate looping controls for handling the creation of the HTML form, as well as recording the entries into that form.

When it comes to file handling, there are still many more options that you can look at on the PHP website (*http://php.net/index.php*). If you go to the "Filesystem" section of the manual, you will find a list of over 70 functions—including, of course, the ones discussed here. You can check to see if a file is either readable or writable with the is_readable() or is_writable() functions, respectively. You can check on file permissions, free disk space, or total disk space, and you can delete files, copy files, and much more. When you get right down to it, if you have enough time and desire, you can even write an entire web application without ever needing or using a database system.

When the day comes (and it most likely will) that you have a client who does not want to pay big bucks for the use of a database engine, you will have an alternative approach to offer them.

CHAPTER 8

PHP and Friends

PHP is a wonderful language—it is robust and flexible and friendly. By *friendly*, I mean that it can freely integrate with libraries built by outside sources. This is in keeping with an important and ever-present caveat in the open source development world: not re-inventing the wheel. There are many different libraries out on the Web that can integrate well with PHP and are actually also developed in PHP. In this chapter, we will look at three different PHP add-on libraries and discuss how to use existing tools to enhance our PHP web development.

The three libraries we'll cover are all PHP object-oriented-based, so be sure you have read Chapter 6 in this book or are familiar with object-oriented programming before going too far into the examples. These three libraries were chosen because they are helpful for performing some of the top tasks in a modern web-based application: sending email messages or Short Message Service (SMS) text messages, generating PDF forms, and generating graphical data reports (e.g., pie charts and bar charts).

Email/SMS Generation

PHP has a built-in mail function called `mail()`. This will send out Simple Mail Transport Protocol (SMTP) mail to the world. The mail function is quite simplistic and basic, so it usually is not the best choice, on its own, for heavier email tasks. It's tricky to send email messages with attachments, for example.

The PHP library, called PHPMailer, is just what the doctor ordered to fill the gap. It is object-based and you can add it easily into a script with either an `include` or, more appropriately, a `require` command. You can find the PHPMailer library at the following URL: *http://phpmailer.worxware.com/index.php?pg=phpmailer*.

If you have control over your server and where files are to be located, you should consider placing this library in a commonly accessible folder so that all of your PHP applications can share access to it, thus preventing multiple installations of the same library. This will also help with maintaining the most current version of the library across all of your websites. If you want the library to be available to all PHP files, you can move the *class.phpmailer.php* file into your *php.ini* include path. This is true for all the libraries that are covered in this chapter.

After you have made reference to the `PHPMailer` class with a `require` command, simply instantiate the class and start using it. Consider the following simple example taken from the PHPMailer installation guide:

```
require("class.phpmailer.php");

$mail = new PHPMailer();

// set mailer to use SMTP
$mail->IsSMTP();
// specify main and backup server
$mail->Host = "smtp1.example.com;smtp2.example.com";
// turn on SMTP authentication
$mail->SMTPAuth = true;
// SMTP username
$mail->Username = "petermac";
// SMTP password
$mail->Password = "secret";

$mail->From = "from@example.com";
$mail->FromName = "Mailer";

// name is optional
$mail->AddAddress("josh@example.net", "Josh Adams");
$mail->AddAddress("ellen@example.com");
$mail->AddReplyTo("info@example.com", "Information");

// set word wrap to 50 characters
$mail->WordWrap = 50;
// add attachments
$mail->AddAttachment("/var/tmp/file.tar.gz");
// optional attachment file name
$mail->AddAttachment("/tmp/image.jpg", "new.jpg");
// set email format to HTML
$mail->IsHTML(true);

$mail->Subject = "Here is the subject";

$mail->Body    = "This is the HTML message
body <b>in bold!</b>";

$mail->AltBody = "This is the body in plain text for
non-HTML mail clients";
```

```
if(!$mail->Send())
{
    echo "Message could not be sent. <p>";
    echo "Mailer Error: " . $mail->ErrorInfo;
} else {
    echo "Message has been sent";
}
```

As you can see, it's pretty straightforward to build and send an email message, even with attachments. One thing you can also do here is to use the `$mail->AddAddress` method within a `while` loop to send a stock email message to a list of recipients from your database records. If you are going to be doing a lot of email generation with different aspects to the messages, be sure to get to know the methods of this class very well so that you can be efficient with your code. Remember, though, that nobody likes spam!

Sending out an SMS or text message to a cell phone is just as simple as sending out a regular email message. Using the same PHPMailer library, you just need to make a few simple adjustments so that you are sending information to a phone rather than to an email account. Naturally, you have to know the phone number of the recipient and it is best to have the permission of the recipient to send her a text message. Maintaining this information in a database is, again, very convenient; just be sure you have that permission.

Next, you need the address of the recipient's SMS provider, the *SMS domain*. In Canada, for example, there is Bell Aliant, Rogers, and Telus, and their respective SMS addresses are: @txt.bell.ca, @pcs.rogers.com, and @msg.telus.com. Each provider should have this domain address readily available on its website.

Here is some sample code that shows a text message being generated and sent:

```
if($OK_to_SMS) {

    $SMSPhoneNum = str_replace('-', '',$CellNumber);

    $sql = <<<SQL
SELECT SMSDomain
FROM SMSProvider
WHERE SMSProviderID = '$SMSProviderID'
SQL;

    $db = new mysqli(
        "localhost",      // database server
        $db_username,     // username
        $db_password,     // password
        $db_name )        // database name
        or die("Cannot connect to server. Error code: %s\n" .
         mysqli_connect_errno());

    $result = $db->query($sql) or die("Could not execute SQL: $sql");
    $row = $result->fetch_assoc();
```

```
$body = "Dear $Fname $Lname: \r\n \r\n"
. "We would like to inform you that you have been selected for jury duty. "
. "Check your email at $ContactEmail for more detailed information.";

$mail = new PHPMailer();
$mail->IsSMTP();
$mail->SMTPAuth = true;

$mail->Host = "localhost";
$mail->From = "notification@juryduty.com";
$mail->FromName = "Law Courts of Anytown";
$mail->AddAddress($SMSPhoneNum . $row['SMSDomain']);
$mail->Body = $body;
$mail->WordWrap = 50;

if(!$mail->Send()) {
    echo "Jury duty notification not sent: SMS <br/>";
    echo "Mailer Error: " . $mail->ErrorInfo . "<br/>";
} else {
    echo "Jury duty notification sent";
}
}
```

Notice here that we first verify that it is OK to SMS message the recipient. We then do a string replacement on the phone number to take out any dashes. You should also do this for brackets around the area code, if they exist. This is so that the SMS phone number will be in the correct format: just numbers, no punctuation. Then we prepare the text message in a very similar fashion as before and send it as email to the concatenated phone number and SMS provider domain.

 Keep in mind that text messages are generally meant to be short, so you may also want to control the length of the message body by limiting the number of characters.

PDF Generation

Adobe's Portable Document Format (PDF) files have almost become the standard for preparing well-formatted documents. There are PDF readers/displayers for most web browsers, so there is no real excuse for not providing this kind of formatted document to your users if your web application demands its use. Standardized forms and statistical reports can all be drawn from a web system's data, so it makes sense to format that data in a common layout.

There is a PHP add-on library that allows for the generation of dynamic PDF-formatted output. There are actually a few such PHP libraries out there, but we will look at one of the most widely used libraries, called FPDF (*http://fpdf.org/*). This library is also object-based and you can include it in your scripts the same way that you include the PHPMailer library.

To get started, here is a simple example of some code that will perform three simple tasks: create a blank PDF document, add some text to it, and display it:

```
require("../../fpdf/fpdf.php");

$pdf = new FPDF( );
$pdf->AddPage();
$pdf->SetFont('Arial','B',16);
$pdf->Cell(0,10,'PHP - The Good Parts!');
$pdf->Output();
```

As you can see from this code listing, after requiring the library file, we instantiate an object of the FPDF class and call it $pdf. Then we add a page with the AddPage method, set our output font, define the cell (location) for our string of output, and then—using the Output method—display the PDF in the browser. The actual browser output will look like that shown in Figure 8-1.

When building these PDF pages in code you may get the following error:

"FPDF error: Some data has already been output, can't send PDF file."

This just means that there is already some output being sent to the browser. You can either find and remove the extraneous output or work around it by using the ob_start and ob_end_flush function combination at either end of your code listing.

Figure 8-1. Output of simple PHP-generated PDF

There is a concept in FPDF called the document's *cell*. This refers to a rectangular area on the page that you can create and control. The cell can have a height, width, border, and, of course, text. The basic syntax for the cell method is as follows:

```
Cell(float w [, float h [, string txt [, mixed border
    [, int ln [, string align [, int fill [, mixed link]]]]]]])
```

The options for the Cell method call are width of the cell, height of the cell, text to be included in the cell, cell border (if desired), a new line control, alignment of the text within the cell, the cell's fill color (if desired), and an HTML link if the text is to be a link to a web resource.

 If you leave the cell width (first attribute) at 0, the cell will take the entire width of the defined page. This only really becomes apparent when you turn on the border (as shown in the following example) or if you want different-sized cells on the same plane. In the latter case, you would potentially see the text overlapping.

So, for example, if we want to change our original example to have a border and be aligned to the right, we would change the method call to the following:

```
$pdf->Cell(0,10,'PHP - The Good Parts!' ,1 ,0 ,'R');
```

This would produce the browser output shown in Figure 8-2.

Figure 8-2. PHP PDF output right aligned, with border

The `Cell` method is the workhorse for output onto a PDF document and is used extensively while generating PDF documents with FPDF, so you would be well-served if you spent the time needed to learn the ins and outs of this method.

The new line control option of this method (and other FPDF methods) is important to understand. It controls the positioning of the writing cursor after the method is completed. In the above case, it is set to 0, which means that the write cursor will stay on the same line when it is finished and any subsequent writing will also take place from the left margin, potentially causing overlapping of output. If, however, it is set to 1, the write cursor will move to the next line as defined by the height attribute of the previous method call.

There is another FPDF method that comes in handy when you are trying to place separate data on the same output line, and it is called `SetX`. This moves the write cursor from the left margin by a set distance (we will talk about the measurement attributes in the next section). This may sound a little confusing, so let's look at two simple examples with two `Cell` method calls each. The first example will leave the write cursor on the same line, and the second example will move it to the next line.

Here is the code and browser image (Figure 8-3) for the first example:

```
require("../../fpdf/fpdf.php");
```

```
$pdf = new FPDF( );
$pdf->AddPage();
$pdf->SetFont('Arial','B',16);
$pdf->Cell(10,10,'PHP - The Good Parts!', 0,0,'L');
$pdf->SetX(90);
$pdf->Cell(90,10,'Beware the Ides of March!', 1,0,'C');
$pdf->Output();
```

Figure 8-3. PDF output of two text blocks on the same line

 You may want to disable your browser's caching capabilities while you are developing and testing the layout of your FPDF PDFs because some browsers will not reload the page with changes if the changes are so small that they don't register as such with the cache control.

And here is the code and browser output (Figure 8-4) for the second example (we do not need to use the SetX method here, as we are moving the write cursor to the following line as part of the cell method call):

```
require("../../fpdf/fpdf.php");

$pdf = new FPDF( );
$pdf->AddPage();
$pdf->SetFont('Arial','B',16);
$pdf->Cell(10,10,'PHP - The Good Parts!', 0,1,'L');
$pdf->Cell(90,10,'Beware the Ides of March!', 1,0,'C');
$pdf->Output();
```

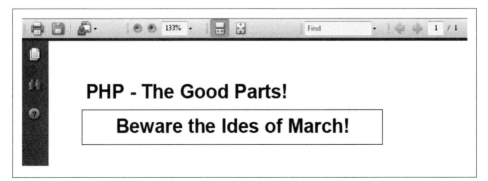

Figure 8-4. PDF output of two text blocks on separate lines

Constructor Method and Basic Document Options

As mentioned earlier, there are different settings for the measurement units on the PDF pages within FPDF. You can control them by sending parameters to the constructor when you instantiate a new copy of the class. Previously, you saw the `$pdf = new FPDF( );` statement of instantiation, which creates an object with the default attributes. You can send the following parameters into the constructor:

- The page orientation has the options of portrait (P) or landscape (L), portrait being the default.
- The units of measurement have the options of point (pt), millimeter (mm), centimeter (cm), and inches (in), with millimeter as the default.
- The page size has the options of A3, A4, A5, Letter, and Legal, with A4 as the default.

Here is a constructor call that defines portrait, inches, and letter layout:

```
$pdf = new FPDF('P', 'in', 'Letter' );
```

 You can even define a custom page layout, if you want, by sending an array of dimensions into the constructor in place of the third parameter. Business cards or special fliers, for instance, could have their own page dimensions. This constructor call will define a page that is 4 × 5 inches and landscape orientation:

```
$pdf = new FPDF('L', 'in', array(4,5));
```

Adding Document Headers and Footers

Let's take a look at object inheritance, or extension, in action. Naturally, there is often a need for headers and footers on a multipage PDF document. FPDF has empty header and footer methods, and they are called automatically each time the `AddPage` method is called. Without extending the class and adding content to our own methods of the same names, however, nothing is visually apparent. So, let's extend the class and add custom page header and footer methods to the child class. Here is the code:

```
require("../../fpdf/fpdf.php");

class myPDF extends FPDF {

    public $title = "FPDF Sample Page Header";

    //Page header method
    function Header() {

        $this->SetFont('Times','',12);
        $w = $this->GetStringWidth($this->title)+150;
        $this->SetDrawColor(0,0,180);
        $this->SetFillColor(170,169,148);
```

```
    $this->SetTextColor(0,0,255);
    $this->SetLineWidth(1);
    $this->Cell($w,9,$this->title,1,1,'C',1);
    $this->Ln(10);

}

//Page footer method
function Footer()      {
    //Position at 1.5 cm from bottom
    $this->SetY(-15);
    $this->SetFont('Arial','I',8);
    $this->Cell(0,10,'page footer -> Page '
        .$this->PageNo().'/{nb}',0,0,'C');
}

}

$pdf = new myPDF('P', 'mm', 'Letter');
$pdf->AliasNbPages();
$pdf->AddPage();
$pdf->SetFont('Times','',24);
$pdf->Cell(0,0,'text at the top of the page',0,0,'L');
$pdf->ln(225);
$pdf->Cell(0,0,'text near page bottom',0,0,'C');
$pdf->AddPage();
$pdf->SetFont('Arial','B',15);
$pdf->Cell(0,0,'Top of page 2 after page header',0,1,'C');
$pdf->Output();
```

There are a number of other methods being called from within the extended header
and footer methods. Some of this is included here to show you that the entire class is
inherited and not just the header and footer methods. Also, some of the methods are
used to show the difference between the header and footer areas distinctly. The full
listing of methods and their uses can be found on the product web page (*http://www
.fpdf.org/*) under the "Manual" link. The image shown in Figure 8-5 is the result of the
above code being executed within the browser. It is a picture of the bottom of one page
(to show the footer) and the top of the next page (to show the header).

 You can suppress the header or footer on a certain page by querying the
value of the page number with the returned value from the PageNo()
method and reacting appropriately. Make sure to use the AliasNb
Pages method before you add your first page to the document so that
FPDF can count the pages being created.

Adding Images and Links

You can also add image and link content to PDF files with the FPDF library. These links
can be anchors within the PDF file itself or full URL resources on the Web. First, we

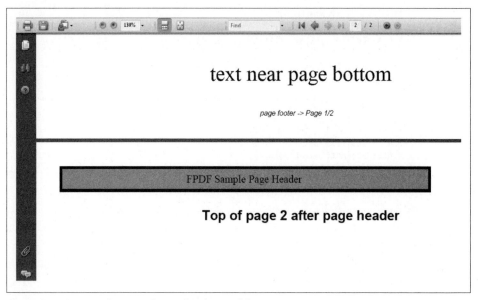

Figure 8-5. Generated PDF with page headers and footers

will look at inserting images into the PDF file, then we will look at making links from either images or text.

To add an image to the document, simply use the image method. In the following code, we will use the image method within the header method to add a PHP logo to the page header and remove the background fill color option from the cell method call so that we can see the image. The image parameters are the image filename, the x and y coordinates of the image, and the width and height of the image:

```
function Header() {

    $this->SetFont('Times','',12);
    $w = $this->GetStringWidth($this->title)+150;
    $this->SetTextColor(0,0,255);
    $this->SetLineWidth(1);
    $this->Image('phplogo.jpg',10,10.5,15,8.5);
    $this->Cell($w,9,$this->title,1,1,'C');
    $this->Ln(10);

}
```

The PDF document now looks like the image shown in Figure 8-6.

Now, to make this image link to the PHP home page, simply add the URL to the last parameter of the image method, skipping the type parameter with a comma.

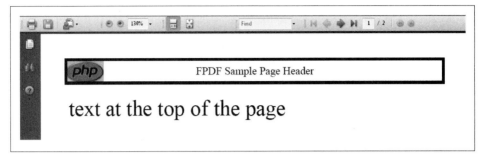

Figure 8-6. Generated PDF with image included in the page header

 It's a good idea to save the URL text to a string variable and then use that in the method parameter listing; this will make it easier to read and possibly reuse if there are other links using the same URL at other places in your document.

The new linking method call now looks like this:

```
$php_url = "http://www.php.net" ;
$this->Image('phplogo.jpg',10,10.5,15,8.5,"",$php_url);
```

The image is now a clickable link image, as shown by the hover text in Figure 8-7.

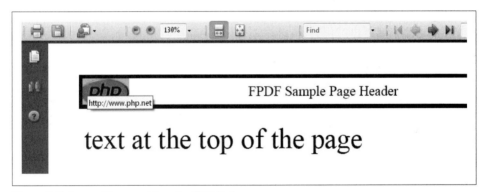

Figure 8-7. Inserted image with active URL link

The other kind of link that we can add to the PDF document is a link to another location within the document. This is the concept of a table of contents or an index. Creating an internal link is done in two parts. First, you define the origin for the link (the link itself), then you set the anchor (the destination that the link will take you to when you click it).

To set the origin of a link, use the AddLink() method. This method returns a handle for use when creating the destination portion of the link with the SetLink() method, which takes the origin's link handle as its parameter so that it can perform the connection between the two items. Here is some sample code that performs the creation of both the origin and the destination parts; notice the use of the FPDF write method, which is another way to send text to the document (as opposed to using the cell method):

```php
require("../../fpdf/fpdf.php");

$pdf = new FPDF();

//First page
$pdf->AddPage();
$pdf->SetFont('Times','',14);

$pdf->write(5,'For a link to page 2 - Click ');
$pdf->SetFont('','U');
$pdf->SetTextColor(0,0,255);
$link_to_pg2 = $pdf->AddLink();
$pdf->write(5,'here',$link_to_pg2);
$pdf->SetFont('');

//Second page
$pdf->AddPage();
$pdf->SetLink($link_to_pg2);
$pdf->Image('phplogo.jpg',10,10,30,0,'','http://www.php.net');
$pdf->ln(20);
$pdf->SetTextColor(1);
$pdf->Cell(0,5,'This is a link and a clickable image', 0, 1, 'L');
$pdf->SetFont('','U');
$pdf->SetTextColor(0,0,255);
$pdf->Write(5,'www.oreilly.com','http://www.oreilly.com');
$pdf->Output();
```

The browser outputs for both the link and the destination page for this code are shown in Figures 8-8 and 8-9.

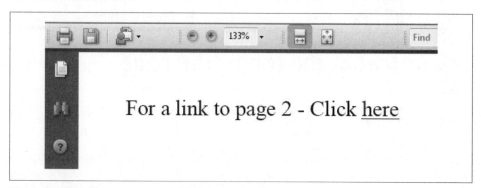

Figure 8-8. PDF document generated with an internal link

Figure 8-9. Anchor page of PDF sample code with additional links

Adding a Watermark

The next feature that we'll look at is making a watermark appear on the PDF document. This can be a nice addition to generated reports or sales brochures that you may want to create within a PHP application. Here is the code to create the watermark:

```
require("../../fpdf/fpdf.php");

$pdf = new FPDF( );
$pdf->AddPage();
$pdf->SetFont('Arial','B',16);
$pdf->SetXY(26,100);
$pdf->image('php_watermark.jpg');
$pdf->SetY(35);
$text = "This is sample text to show the watermark underneath it.";
for($i = 0; $i < 35; $i++) { $pdf->Cell(0,5,$text,0,1); }
$pdf->Output();
```

All that is really going on here is that we are moving the write cursor around the page with the SetXY and SetY methods, and we have an image that is set to a semitransparent shading level. There is really no difference here from setting an image on the page, except that we are overwriting the image with additional text. If this had not been a semitransparent image, the text and the image would be garbled together and it would look like a mess.

Make sure you add the image to the document first in the case of a watermark, as the last items sent to the document will overwrite anything previously sent. In Figure 8-10, if the text were sent out first, followed by the image, the image would overlay the text.

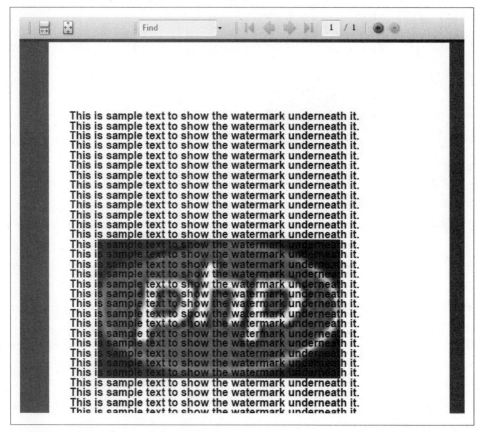

Figure 8-10. PDF with generated watermark

Dynamic PDFs and Table Display

Now we want to really make FPDF earn its keep. Up to this point, we have only been sending static information to the PDFs being created. Let's look at how to integrate a PDF document with database information drawn out by a query request. We will display that information in a nicely formatted table on the PDF itself, thus making the PDF dynamic in its content. The following code listing is a little long, but it is well commented and the highlights are discussed in the subsequent paragraphs:

```php
require("../../fpdf/fpdf.php");

class PDF extends FPDF {

    function BuildTable($header,$data) {
        //Colors, line width and bold font
        $this->SetFillColor(255,0,0);
        $this->SetTextColor(255);
        $this->SetDrawColor(128,0,0);
        $this->SetLineWidth(.3);
```

```php
        $this->SetFont('','B');
        //Header
        // make an array for the column widths
        $w=array(85,40,15);
        // send the headers to the PDF document
        for($i=0;$i<count($header);$i++)
            $this->Cell($w[$i],7,$header[$i],1,0,'C',1);
        $this->Ln();
        //Color and font restoration
        $this->SetFillColor(175);
        $this->SetTextColor(0);
        $this->SetFont('');

        //now spool out the data from the $data array
        $fill=true;  // used to alternate row color backgrounds
        foreach($data as $row)
        {
            $this->Cell($w[0],6,$row[0],'LR',0,'L',$fill);
            // set colors to show a URL style link
            $this->SetTextColor(0,0,255);
            $this->SetFont('', 'U');
            $this->Cell($w[1],6,$row[1],'LR',0,'L',$fill, 'http://www.oreilly.com');
            // restore normal color settings
            $this->SetTextColor(0);
            $this->SetFont('');
            $this->Cell($w[2],6,$row[2],'LR',0,'C',$fill);

            $this->Ln();
            // flips from true to false and vise versa
            $fill =! $fill;
        }
        $this->Cell(array_sum($w),0,'','T');
    }
}

//connect to database
$connection = mysql_connect("localhost","user", "password");
$db = "library";
mysql_select_db($db, $connection)
    or die( "Could not open $db database");


$sql = 'SELECT * FROM books ORDER BY pub_year';
$result = mysql_query($sql, $connection)
    or die( "Could not execute sql: $sql");

// build the data array from the database records.
While($row = mysql_fetch_array($result)) {
    $data[] = array($row['title'], $row['ISBN'], $row['pub_year'] );
}

// start and build the PDF document
$pdf = new PDF();

//Column titles
```

```
$header=array('Book Title','ISBN','Year');

$pdf->SetFont('Arial','',14);
$pdf->AddPage();
// call the table creation method
$pdf->BuildTable($header,$data);
$pdf->Output();
```

In this code, we use the database connection and build two arrays to send to the `BuildTable()` custom method of this extended class. Inside the `BuildTable()` method, we set colors and font attributes for the table header, then send out the headers based on the first array passed in. An array called `$w` (for width) sets the column widths and is used in the calls to the `cell()` methods.

After the table header is sent out, we use the `$data` array that contains the database information and walk through that array with a `foreach` loop. Notice here that the `cell()` method uses `LR` for its border parameter. This refers to borders on the left and right of the cell in question, thus effectively adding the sides to the table rows. We also add a URL link to the second column just to show that it can be done in connection with the table row construction. Finally, we use a `$fill` variable to flip back and forth so that the background color will alternate as the table is constructed row by row.

The final call to the `cell()` method in this `BuildTable()` method draws the bottom of the table and closes off the columns.

The result of executing this code in a browser is shown in Figure 8-11.

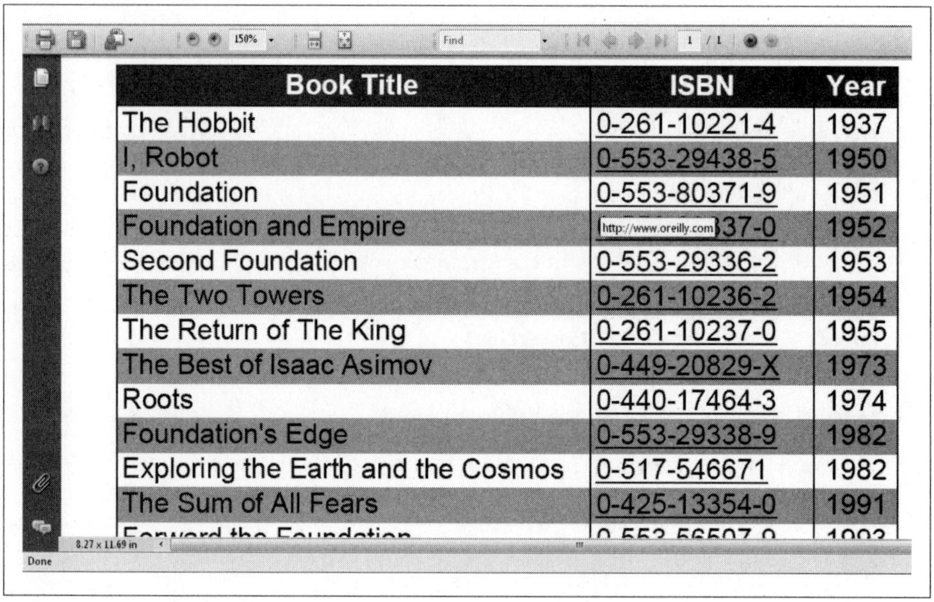

Book Title	ISBN	Year
The Hobbit	0-261-10221-4	1937
I, Robot	0-553-29438-5	1950
Foundation	0-553-80371-9	1951
Foundation and Empire	http://www.oreilly.com 37-0	1952
Second Foundation	0-553-29336-2	1953
The Two Towers	0-261-10236-2	1954
The Return of The King	0-261-10237-0	1955
The Best of Isaac Asimov	0-449-20829-X	1973
Roots	0-440-17464-3	1974
Foundation's Edge	0-553-29338-9	1982
Exploring the Earth and the Cosmos	0-517-546671	1982
The Sum of All Fears	0-425-13354-0	1991

Figure 8-11. Table data taken from MySQL placed in a dynamic PDF

Graphical Reports Generation

JPGraph (*http://www.aditus.nu/jpgraph/*) is used to make graphical statistical reports like bar charts and pie charts. It is an object-oriented code library, so by now it should be fairly straightforward for you to use. As before, you access this library with a `require` statement.

Typically, a graphical report will ask the user for input in order to build the report. This is information like the date range that the report will cover, the sorting order of the data, and so on. In our samples, however, we will simply provide arrays with preset values to make them a little easier to review.

Pie Charts

The first sample graph that we will look at is a pie chart. In the following listing you will see an array of data to be plotted on the chart assigned to a variable called `$data`; this is the data that would normally be provided by a data entry page, a `select` statement from a database, or a combination of both. We can do this after we bring in the appropriate libraries for the chart that we are about to build.

JPGraph is a little different than other libraries in the sense that there is a basic library required by all graphs being generated, as well as individual specialized libraries, or sublibraries, that are more suited to each graph type. In this case, we use the *jpgraph_pie.php* file because we are creating a pie chart. After we reference the correct libraries and provide the raw data, we instantiate the `$piechart` class from the `Pie Graph` object and pass two numbers representing the width and height of the chart to the constructor. Then we simply start using the methods available to us to build the chart.

We can control the look of the title of the chart by setting the title text, its font, and its colors. Then we instantiate an object called `$pPlot`, which is a rendition of the pie shape itself and how it is sliced up based on the `$data` array we built earlier. Next, we can describe the labels that will accompany each slice of the pie. Finally, we add the plotted chart onto the graph with the `Add` method, and display the whole thing with the `Stroke` method:

```
include ("../../jpgraph/jpgraph.php");
include ("../../jpgraph/jpgraph_pie.php");

$data = array(12, 15, 23, 18, 5);

// Create the Pie Graph.
$piechart = new PieGraph(300,350);

// Set a title for the plot
$piechart->title->Set("Sample Pie Chart");
$piechart->title->SetFont(FF_VERDANA,FS_BOLD,12);
$piechart->title->SetColor("darkblue");
```

```
$piechart->legend->Pos(0.1,0.2);

// Create pie plot
$pPlot = new PiePlot($data);
$pPlot->SetCenter(0.5,0.55);
$pPlot->SetSize(0.3);

// Setup the labels
$pPlot->SetLabelType(PIE_VALUE_PER);
$pPlot->value->Show();
$pPlot->value->SetFont(FF_ARIAL,FS_NORMAL,9);
$pPlot->value->SetFormat('%2.1f%%');

// Add and stroke
$piechart->Add($pPlot);
$piechart->Stroke();
```

 The time function is added here to trigger a difference in the browser's cache registration so that the same file can be used by many concurrent users of the same web page.

This code will send the graph shown in Figure 8-12 to the browser. Remember that you can augment this display with other HTML markup if desired.

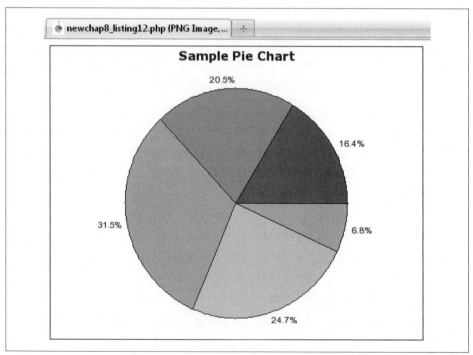

Figure 8-12. Pie chart generated by JPGraph and PHP

If you decide to add additional formatting to the output of the graph, you will have to save the generated graphic as a file and pivot it to the server's hard drive for later display with the accompanying HTML. The stroke method used to generate the graph has an option to name the file and save it for you. The code to save the graphic is:

```
$graph->Stroke("graph.jpg");
```

And the code to bring the graphic back to combine with HTML code is:

```
echo ('<img src="graph.jpg?' .time(). '">');
```

Bar Charts

Another type of chart that we can create is a bar chart. Again, here we will provide the benchmark values to the graph directly for easier code review. The code for this sample follows, and you will see that it uses the specific sublibrary for bar charts to work properly. Other than the proper selection of the sublibrary, there is really not too much difference in the approach—there are specific methods used, but the concept is basically the same. Here is the code:

```
include ("../../jpgraph/jpgraph.php");
include ("../../jpgraph/jpgraph_bar.php");
include ("../../jpgraph/jpgraph_line.php");

// We need some data
$datay=array(31,44,49,40,24,47,12);

// Set up the graph
$graph = new Graph(600,300,"auto");
$graph->img->SetMargin(60,30,30,40);
$graph->SetScale("textlin");
$graph->SetMarginColor("teal");
$graph->SetShadow();

// Create the bar pot
$bplot = new BarPlot($datay);
$bplot->SetWidth(0.6);

// Set up color for gradient fill style
$tcol=array(100,100,255);
$fcol=array(255,100,100);
$bplot->SetFillGradient($fcol,$tcol,GRAD_VERT);
$bplot->SetFillColor("orange");
$graph->Add($bplot);

// Set up the title for the graph
$graph->title->Set("Sample Bargraph");
$graph->title->SetColor("yellow");
$graph->title->SetFont(FF_VERDANA,FS_BOLD,12);

// Set up color for axis and labels
$graph->xaxis->SetColor("black","white");
```

```
$graph->yaxis->SetColor("black","white");

// Set up font for axis
$graph->xaxis->SetFont(FF_VERDANA,FS_NORMAL,10);
$graph->yaxis->SetFont(FF_VERDANA,FS_NORMAL,10);
$graph->yaxis->title->Set("Value Range");
$graph->yaxis->title->SetColor("white");
$graph->yaxis->title->SetFont(FF_VERDANA,FS_NORMAL,10);

// Set up X-axis title (color & font)
$graph->xaxis->title->Set("item Count");
$graph->xaxis->title->SetColor("white");
$graph->xaxis->title->SetFont(FF_VERDANA,FS_NORMAL,10);

// Finally send the graph to the browser
$graph->Stroke();
```

Figure 8-13 shows the chart that this code produces.

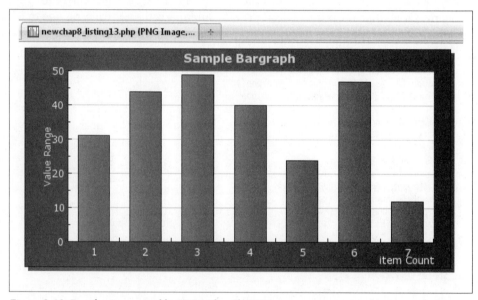

Figure 8-13. Bar chart generated by JPGraph and PHP

Captchas

One last quick sample is in order. If you have ever ordered concert tickets online, you will be familiar with the kind of antispam image shown in Figure 8-14.

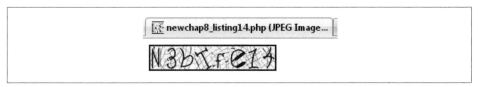

Figure 8-14. Antispam graphic generated by JPGraph and PHP

JPGraph can generate this kind of captcha in just a few lines of code, and the supplied characters can be either provided manually (by you) or generated randomly:

```
require_once "../../jpgraph/jpgraph_antispam.php";

$spam = new AntiSpam();
// saved to $chars for later verification of correct entry
$chars = $spam->Rand(8);
$spam->Stroke() ;
```

Be sure to visit the website for this library and review all the other options that it provides. You can add background images to the graphs, adjust the grid lines behind the bars, and so much more. Many other types of charts and graphs are also available, like stock, radar, scatter, polar, and Gantt charts.

CHAPTER 9

PHP Security

In today's world of identity theft and credit card fraud, it is imperative for websites to be as secure as possible. It has been proven time and again that nothing is 100 percent foolproof in the security field, so it behooves (I've always wanted to use that word in a book) us to be as diligent as possible in protecting the information and websites that have been placed in our trust. When using PHP, there are a number of best practices to follow in an attempt to mitigate the risks.

The most vulnerable portions of a website are any places where data is entered or manipulated. Although that sounds vague and indicates a potentially large target area, I really mean to make you think about all of the areas in your websites where potential attackers can interact with your site. Let's examine these areas in detail and look at some examples of how you can reduce their vulnerabilities.

Data Validation

Any area of your website that allows for data input is a potential risk area: data entry forms, search inputs, query strings, and so on. The general rule of thumb here is to treat any outside source of data as suspect, and to manage it by filtering it as soon as it becomes available to you. What does filtering mean? Well, once data is passed to your control, you inspect it and alter it if needed—or reject it if it does not meet your input criterion. This is known as validating your data on the most basic of levels. The section "Cross-Site Scripting (XXS) and SQL Injection" on page 115 describes a deeper protection process that you should also follow.

Data can be passed to a form via the `$_GET` and `$_POST` superglobal arrays (and their "parent" entity, `$_REQUEST`). Data can also be sent to a website through `$_COOKIE` and `$_SESSION` arrays. Let's look at how to handle this information in a general sense. You will have to know where the data will come from (a form that you created), otherwise that information will remain harmless. If, for example, there is malicious data in the `$_COOKIE` array but you never use it, you are generally safe.

When "*catching*" (or intercepting) submitted data, arrays are just right for the job, so be sure to always initialize an empty array at the beginning of your code. That way, you will be sure that its genesis is always clean and under your control. In fact, it is always good practice to initiate your variables; this gives you control over their content from the outset. I use an array named $trusted for this purpose. Let's say you have a basic submission form that will accept a first name, a last name, and a phone number. The first name has to be 35 characters or fewer in length, the last name 45 characters or fewer, and the phone number has to be numeric only and 10 characters in length (no brackets around the area code and no dash after the exchange prefix). This form will use the POST method for submission. Here is the code that will display the form (pure HTML):

```
<html>
<body>
<table>
<form method='post' action='chap8_listing2.php'>
<tr>
    <td> First Name:</td>
    <td> <input type='text' name='firstname' size=35> </td>
</tr>
<tr>
    <td> Last Name:</td>
    <td> <input type='text' name='lastname' size=45> </td>
</tr>
<tr>
    <td> Phone:</td>
    <td> <input type='text' name='phone' size=10> </td>
</tr>
<tr>
    <td colspan=2><input type='submit' value='Submit'></td>
</tr>

</table>
</body>
</html>
```

Here is the code that will accept that submission and filter the input:

```
$trusted = array() ;

if (strlen($_POST['firstname']) <= 35) $trusted['firstname'] =
$_POST['firstname'] ;

if (strlen($_POST['lastname']) <= 45) $trusted['lastname'] = $_POST['lastname'] ;

if (strlen($_POST['phone']) <= 10 && is_numeric($_POST['phone']) ){
    $trusted['phone'] = $_POST['phone'] ;
}

var_dump($trusted) ;
```

When we enter some valid information into each field, the output of the var_dump looks like this:

```
array(3) { ["firstname"]=> string(5) "Peter" ["lastname"]=> string(9)
"MacIntyre" ["phone"]=> string(10) "9025551234" }
```

 This code uses the is_numeric function and not the is_int function for validation, because HTML forms return fields of type "text" as character strings. You can see this in the output, where the phone element in the array is listed with a data type of string(10). If you really want to test for numerical data, cast the incoming data to an integer data type first.

There are many other methods of data validation or manipulation you can use, such as forcing the initial letter in a name field to be capitalized (ucfirst PHP function), forcing uppercase for all in a provided string (ucwords PHP function), requiring a field to contain data (if ($fname == "") { //raise an error }), and so on. It is impossible to go through all possible validation methods here, since they depend on the data being collected in the form and what you plan to do with that data once it is collected. The point here is that there is some data interception and possible massaging being done on data that is provided to your web pages from an outside (untrusted) source. Although this is not purely a security programming technique, it certainly helps with data integrity. It also helps to ensure that your data is in pristine condition before it is saved to a database.

Escape Output

The other side of the coin in web data security is preparing your information to be sent out to one of two destinations (generally): to the web browser as display output or to a database as storage output (to a database engine). It is a common mistake to think that because the data is yours and you filtered it when you received it, it is free from error and therefore will be just fine to send as output. Remember the caveat that is the security mantra: never completely trust your data, even if it is yours. In other words, "better safe than sorry."

So the first area of output that we will look at is sending data to a browser. Remember, PHP is basically an HTML generator: the actual code that shows on the user's browser when you display the source is raw HTML. To help PHP turn out proper HTML, we can use the htmlspecialchars function. This function turns relevant data into its respective HTML equivalent, thus rendering it as raw output rather than actionable HTML code. Here is an example:

```
$string = "'Fred' & 'Barney' <a href='http://www.abadsite.com'>
click here, you know you want to</a>" ;
// note the single quotes.

echo htmlspecialchars($string);
echo "<br/>" ;
echo htmlspecialchars($string, ENT_QUOTES);
```

Notice that the second call to `htmlspecialchars` uses a second parameter of a defined constant. This tells PHP how to deal with any quotation marks that may be embedded within the string. Table 9-1 lists the options that you can use with this parameter.

Table 9-1. Defined constant options for htmlspecialchars function

Defined constant	Effect of use
ENT_COMPAT (default)	Will convert double quotes and leave single quotes alone.
ENT_QUOTES	Will convert both double and single quotes.
ENT_NOQUOTES	Will leave both double and single quotes unconverted.

The browser output of this string is:

```
'Fred' & 'Barney' <a href='http://www.abadsite.com'>click here,
               you know you want to</a>
'Fred' & 'Barney' <a href='http://www.abadsite.com'>click here,
               you know you want to</a>
```

And the revealed source code display looks like this:

```
'Fred' &amp; 'Barney' &lt;a href='http://www.abadsite.com'&gt;
click here, you know you want to&lt;/a&gt;
<br/>
&#039;Fred&#039; &amp; &#039;Barney&#039; &lt;a href=&#039;
http://www.abadsite.com&#039;&gt;click here, you know you want to&lt;/a&gt;
```

As you can see, if someone were attempting to insert a link into your site, it would merely be displayed as text output and the link would not be active (clickable).

> `htmlspecialchars` only acts on the most common forms of HTML elements. These are ampersand (&), double quotes, single quotes, greater than (>), and less than (<) characters. If you want to be extra cautious, you can use the more comprehensive `htmlentities` function, which covers all of the HTML elements.

The next most common destination for output in a PHP application is a database; most PHP sites will use MySQL for their data stores. PHP provides a function that will escape your data so that it is ready for database activity: `mysql_real_escape_string`. As your SQL commands are sent to the database as a constructed string, there is always the potential that the SQL command string will be abnormally ended by your content. Consider an example in which you are inserting "O'Mally" as a last name into a string like this:

```
$sql = "UPDATE team SET name = 'O'Mally' WHERE teamid = 15" ;
```

Without the escape, this string will actually trigger an error response when it is sent to the database, because the intervening single quote will terminate the string before you want it to. This is even harder to predict when that last name data is coming from a variable source. Here is the error response:

```
ERROR: Unclosed quote @ 31
STR: '
SQL: UPDATE team SET name = 'O'Mally' WHERE teamid = 15
```

The solution is to run the data that will be part of your SQL string through the `mysql_real_escape_string` function before you send it to the database. Your code should look something like this:

```
// actually need a db connection established before this will work.
$conn = mysql_connect("localhost","dbuser","password");
$db = "dbname";
mysql_select_db($db, $conn) or die( "Could not open $db");

$trusted['lname'] = mysql_real_escape_string("O'Mally") ;
$sql = "UPDATE team SET name = '$trusted[lname]' WHERE teamid = 15" ;

mysql_query($sql);
```

 `mysql_real_escape_string` is specific to the MySQL database engine. There are equivalent functions for other database engines for which PHP has drivers. Prepared statements in PDO also have this ability with the `quote()` function. If a database is in use that does not have its own native `real_escape_string` function, you can use the generic function called `addslashes`.

Once this is done, the string will look like this before it is sent to the database, with the problematic quotation mark escaped with a backslash:

```
UPDATE team SET name = 'o\'mally' WHERE teamid = 15
```

For more on escaping characters, see "The Great Escape" on page 34.

Cross-Site Scripting (XXS) and SQL Injection

Cross-site scripting and SQL injection occur when an attacker is attempting to inject some code (JavaScript or SQL) into a form on your website. Any data entry point on a form is vulnerable to this type of abuse. Without actually teaching you how to exploit a site, a simple test is to enter the following script into a search box on a website and submit it.

```
<script> alert("howdy") ; </script>
```

If an alert box comes up, the site is not as well protected as it could be. Figure 9-1 shows a site that I found with this exact issue.

 Most injection types of attacks depend on the desire of the attacker to cause your site some pain. The attacker has to spend some time on your site and make some educated guesses as to the nature of your underlying code, so try not to be overly obvious in naming your entities.

Figure 9-1. Browser showing XXS injection vulnerability

The attacker could also attempt to inject additional SQL commands into a form. Entering code like this into a field could expose an SQL injection opportunity:

```
flintstone'; drop table customers;
```

What is being attempted here is the abnormal completion of an SQL command that is naturally part of the website's data processing and the insertion of additional SQL that will cause grief on the site. Now, this raises the point that the attacker would have to know the name of a table in order to make it drop, and you would have to be using the MySQLi multiquery function at the same time, but stranger things have happened. There are a couple ways to protect your site in this particular example. One is to filter the input and not allow any semicolons in the string of text. The other is to ensure that the web user (the credentials that you use in your code to access the database) does not have the right to drop tables.

Using the two methods described in the previous sections (filtering input and escaping output), can almost always thwart these types of attacks.

Password Encryption Security

The last major security issue I'd like to discuss is the encryption of data that you want to ensure is not viewable in its native form. I am talking mostly of user passwords on websites that require clients to log in. There are other examples, such as Social Security (Social Insurance in Canada) numbers, credit card numbers, and so on. The *sha1* encryption algorithm (soon to be upgraded to sha2 level) is the way to go. When employing this encryption function, PHP will convert a supplied string value to a 40-character hexadecimal number. This is known as one-way encryption because there is really no way to reverse the encryption once it is done (but of course that is the whole point). Here is an example:

```
$string = 'myPassword';
echo sha1($string) ;
```

Here is the browser display of the hexadecimal output:

```
5413ee24723bba2c5a6ba2d0196c78b3ee4628d1
```

 Some people have reported weaknesses in sha0 and sha1. However, another algorithm method that has been in popular use (MD5) has been noted to have reproducible exploits, so it is best to use the sha1 method for now and convert to sha2 when that new algorithm becomes available. It is expected sometime in 2012.

If you want another, more secure level of encryption, you can use the "salt and pepper" approach, which means adding hardcoded values to both the front and back of the value that is to be encrypted, and then encrypting the entire string one more time. Having the values hardcoded in this manner makes it more difficult for an attacker to guess the algorithm and its inputs. Here is a sample, followed by its browser output:

```
// this value would normally be provided by a login form
$string = 'myPassword';

$salt = "peter" ;
$pepper = "MacIntyre" ;

echo "Here is the original sha1 encryption: " . sha1($string) ;
echo "<br/>" ;
$salt  = sha1 ($salt) ;
$pepper  = sha1 ($pepper) ;

$string = $salt . $string . $pepper ;
echo "Here is the prepared string about to be further encrypted: " .$string ;
echo "<br/>" ;
echo "Here is the well seasoned encryption: " . sha1($string) ;
```

Output:

```
Here is the original sha1 encryption: 5413ee24723bba2c5a6ba2d0196c78b3ee4628d1
Here is the prepared string about to be further encrypted:
4b8373d016f277527198385ba72fda0feb5da015myPassword0f1d5a3227a9ce2b3bf67178b6ba
6e5264149a26
Here is the well seasoned encryption: 6dc853b97b4998340b28a84ba714299af1bddadf
```

Security Tips

Finally, here is a quick list of additional things you can do with your PHP environment to help mitigate some vulnerabilities and to avoid providing more information to potential attackers than necessary. Most of these assume that you have full control over your environment. If you do not have this level of control, talk to your hosting provider or change some of the *php.ini* settings on the fly as your code runs.

- Turn off error display (do use the error log) in the *php.ini* file.
- Make sure `register_globals` is turned off in the *php.ini* file (see the Appendix for more detail on this).
- Use secure socket layer (SSL) certificates on your sites where required.
- Keep your included library, SQLite files (if in use), and settings files outside your document root (so that they are not accessible via the web server).

If you would like to explore the topic in a bit more depth, I fully recommend Chris Shiflett's book *Essential PHP Security (http://oreilly.com/catalog/9780596006563/)* (O'Reilly) and Ilia Alshanetsky's *php|architect's Guide to PHP Security* (Marco Tabini & Associates, Inc.) for more comprehensive coverage.

CHAPTER 10

PHP 5.3 Good Parts

PHP 5.3 was released in June 2009. It was a long time in the making and there are quite a few improvements and additions to PHP in this release. Some of the additions to the language were meant for version 6, but since version 6 seemed to be taking a while to come together, it was decided to release the features that were already complete and buy a little more time for version 6 as an added bonus. This chapter will briefly discuss some of the best improvements version 5.3 has to offer.

There was a cornucopia (I have always wanted to use that word in a book, too) of enhancements made to PHP 5.3. Since these enhancements cover the entire PHP product spectrum, we will jump around to a few different concepts here. For example, namespaces primarily affect the object-oriented aspects of PHP while NOWDOC affects management and display of strings. If any of these topics seems confusing, please refer back to earlier sections of the book.

Namespaces

Namespaces are meant to help with potential naming clashes within different object-oriented and function libraries that may be in use within a single development project. You may have libraries from outside sources and libraries that you develop yourself, and two or more of these libraries may have similarly named classes or functions. You might have a PDF-generation library and an email-generation library, both with a function named `Generate`. Without a whole lot of customization programming (and how do you decide which class to alter?), you would be in a real mess. The use of a namespace for each of these classes can help alleviate the problem. The concept is similar to that of a hard drive: you can't have two files of the same name in the same folder (directory), but you can have files of the same name in separate folders—in effect, this is what namespaces do for PHP. In fact, the process of making reference to these namespaces is also similar in that they are referenced with assistance of the backslash (\) character (more on this later).

There are some rules around creating a namespaces, and they are quite strict:

1. There cannot be any code in the file before the declaration of the first namespace (no HTML, no whitespace, nothing). OK, there are actually two exceptions: you can have comments and you can use the declare statement to define constants within the code file if you like.
2. You must use the keyword namespace.
3. The namespace must have a unique name, and you cannot use an existing PHP keyword.
4. Once a namespace is employed, all other code must be defined within a namespace.

Here is an example (I am including the PHP tags here to show that Rule 1 is being honored):

```php
<?php
namespace Sample1 ;

    function sayHello($name) {
        echo "Hello there: " . $name ;
    }

echo "This is a test <br/>" ;

sayHello("Johnny") ;
?>
```

This will produce the output of:

```
This is a test
Hello there: Johnny
```

At first glance, our sample code may not appear to be following rule 4; however, once the namespace Sample1 is defined, all the code following is actually part of that namespace.

It is also possible to define more than one namespace and to have an open or global namespace. This is where we get to work around like-named entities. I should also mention that a better way to define namespaces is to use curly braces ({ and }) around the contents of the namespace. So we can rewrite the code above as follows:

```php
<?php
namespace Sample1 {

    function sayHello($name) {
        echo "Hello there: " . $name ;
    }

echo "This is a test <br/>" ;

sayHello("Johnny") ;
}
?>
```

This produces the exact same output as before. It is recommended that you use the curly brace method for defining multiple namespaces, because it helps to visually set them apart and makes the code easier to follow. Once you begin to use multiple namespaces, however, you must also define a global namespace—this is rule 4 coming into play once more. Consider these two code files; the first (*chap9_listing2.php*) has two namespaces defined and will be included in the second file. The second code file defines a global namespace (a namespace without an identifier) for the main body of the code, but makes use of (references) the code within the included namespace definitions.

```php
<?php
// this is file: chap9_listing2.php
namespace Sample1 {

    function sayHello($name) {
        echo "Hello there: " . $name ;
    }
}

namespace Sample2 {

function sayHello($name) {
        echo "I am happy to make your acquaintance " . $name ;
    }
}

?>
<?php
// this is file: chap9_listing3.php
namespace {
    function sayHello($name) {
        echo "greetings from the global scope: " . $name ;
    }

include "chap9_listing2.php" ;

Sample1\sayHello("Frank");
echo "<br/>" ;
Sample2\sayHello("Peter");

echo "<br/>" ;
use Sample1 as S1;
S1\sayHello("Frank");
echo "<br/>" ;
Sample2\sayHello("Peter");

echo "<br/>" ;
sayHello("Charlie") ;
}
?>
```

Notice that the global namespace encompasses the other two namespaces and that it is also possible to add comments to the code before the namespace declaration (a caveat to rule 1: comments do not count as code). The output for this code is:

Hello there: Frank
I am happy to make your acquaintance Peter
Hello there: Frank
I am happy to make your acquaintance Peter
greetings from the global scope: Charlie

As you can see, calling the same named function within different namespaces produces different output. The best way to reference entities within a namespace is to prefix the entity call with the identifier of the namespace separated by a backslash (\) character. Namespaces can be embedded within other namespaces, thus adding additional levels of complexity. Each level of the namespace is separated by another backslash (\) character. So if `Sample1` has another namespace called `email_code` and a function inside that called `sendEmail`, we would reference that function like this:

```
Sample1\email_code\sendEmail() ;
```

Notice in the lower section of *chap9_listing3.php* there are these two lines of code:

```
use Sample1 as S1;
S1\sayHello("Frank");
```

Here we are using another neat feature of namespaces: aliasing. If you are using code from an outside source that is beyond your control, and it has a long or strange name, you can give it your own name through this aliasing feature. Here, we alias the `Sample1` namespace to a shorter reference of `S1`, then call its `sayHello` function.

The final line of code, `sayHello("Charlie")` ; is called without any namespace prefix, which is how references to the global namespace are called.

Closures (Anonymous Functions)

Another addition to PHP 5.3 is known as a *closure*, or *anonymous function*. This concept allows you to create functions with no specified names. We can assign an anonymous function to a variable, as in the following example (notice the assignment is true to the rules of variable assignments in that it requires the ending semicolon):

```
$person_info = function($name, $age, $eyecolor)
{
    echo "greetings: " . $name . "<br/>";
    echo "You are : " . $age . " years old<br/>";
    echo "and your eye color is: " . $eyecolor . "<br/><br/>";
};

$person_info('Peter', '43', 'brown');
$person_info('Dawn', '15', 'green');
```

We assign an unnamed function (closure) to a variable called `$person_info` and expect parameters for it—$name, $age, and $eyecolor. Then we can simply make reference to that variable and pass it values, almost like calling an actual function.

The PHP documentation points out that closures are also great for use in callback functions when you are walking through an array (for example) and you want to run a function against each element of an array. Here is a very simple example:

```php
$person_info = function($value, $key)
{
    echo $key . ": " . $value . "<br/>";
};

$person_array = array('name' => 'Dawn', 'age' => '15', 'eyecolor' => 'green');

array_walk($person_array, $person_info);
```

Here, we pass an actual variable to the `array_walk` function as its second parameter, rather than as a true reference to a function.

NOWDOC

The next 5.3 enhancement I'd like to bring to your attention is called NOWDOC, which is merely a variation on the HEREDOC functionality in relation to string management. If you recall, HEREDOC text behaves the same as if you were working with a string within double quotes, in that it allows for the inclusion of variable content directly within the string such that the content of the variable will be resolved within the string. The NOWDOC construct behaves the same as if you were dealing with strings in single quotes, in that there is *no* resolution of variable content (no interpolation), as the token is defined with single quotes. Here is an example of HEREDOC and NOWDOC to contrast what each does:

```php
$myname = "Peter MacIntyre" ;

$str = <<<"HEREDOC_Example"
Lorem ipsum dolor sit amet,
nibh euismod tincidunt $myname .
HEREDOC_Example;

echo $str ;

$str2 = <<<'NOWDOC_Example'
Lorem ipsum dolor sit amet,
nibh euismod tincidunt $myname .
NOWDOC_Example;

echo "<br/>" . $str2 ;
```

And here is the expected browser output:

Lorem ipsum dolor sit amet, nibh euismod tincidunt Peter MacIntyre.
Lorem ipsum dolor sit amet, nibh euismod tincidunt $myname.

The NOWDOC construct lends itself to longer segments of text that don't require any character or variable escaping, like the body of a standard email message or some disclaimer text on a report.

goto Operator

If you have ever used a language like Basic or Visual Basic, you know all about the goto statement in those languages. There was reportedly a great struggle within the PHP development team when discussing whether they should add this feature to the language, and it looks like the advocates won out. This operator allows you to jump to other locations within a code file. This is a powerful new addition to the language, which is why I am introducing it here. But, as you will see in the following examples, it can also be considered a "bad part" of PHP if used improperly. There is a section on the goto statement in the Appendix for this reason.

There are some limitations on goto's use:

- You cannot jump to another code file.
- You cannot jump out of or into a function or method (you can only jump within the same scope).
- You cannot jump into looping structures like while loops or switch constructs, but you can jump out of them.

To define a goto destination, mark it with a label (which can be alphanumeric, but must start with an alpha character) followed by a colon (:). To activate the jumping action, simply precede the label name with the goto command. Here is a simple example:

```
$letter = "A" ;
if ($letter == "A") {
    goto landing_area_a;
} else {
    goto landing_area_b;
}

landing_area_a:
echo 'The Eagle has landed<br/>';

landing_area_b:
echo 'The Hawk has landed<br/>';
```

The browser output may not be quite what you expect:

```
The Eagle has landed
The Hawk has landed
```

The reason that both of these comments are sent to the browser is that once you reach your goto destination, the code continues from that point and runs forward, so the next label (landing_area_b:) is ignored, but the echo statement is executed, as it is next in line. A way around this is to add another **goto** statement that will effectively jump over the remaining code that you don't want to run.

```
landing_area_a:
echo 'The Eagle has landed<br/>';
goto lands_end;

landing_area_b:
echo 'The Hawk has landed<br/>';

lands_end:
```

Of course, you are starting to see exactly why there was so much discussion about whether or not to add this feature into PHP 5.3. There is the potential to write what is known as *spaghetti code*, code that potentially jumps and lands all over the file and that makes it frightfully difficult to follow and maintain.

One further warning is the potential for endless looping. Take a look at this code and try to follow it; I don't recommend that you load it into your PHP environment unless you have the ability to shut it down on your own:

```
starting_point:
$letter = "A" ;
if ($letter == "A") {
    goto landing_area_a;
} else {
    goto landing_area_b;
}

landing_area_a:
echo 'The Eagle has landed<br/>';
goto lands_end;

landing_area_b:
echo 'The Hawk has landed<br/>';

lands_end:
goto starting_point;
```

Here are the first few lines of the browser output:

```
The Eagle has landed
The Eagle has landed
The Eagle has landed
The Eagle has landed
The Eagle has landed
The Eagle has landed
```

As you can see, this is the dreaded endless loop, which the **goto** operator can create if you are not careful. If this happens to you and you are quick enough on the mouse, you should be able to stop the browser page before it overloads your web server.

Whatever you do, try not to write these two lines of code (I have actually seen an inept programmer write code exactly like this a few years back in a mainframe language):

```
landing15:
goto landing15;
```

It is the tightest possible goto loop, and the hardest one to locate! At least in this instance, PHP gives you all the rope you need and it's up to you not to hang yourself. You have been warned!

DateTime and DateTimeZone Classes

PHP developers should be well aware of the date and time functions that are available for performing date-related tasks like adding a date stamp to a database record entry or calculating the difference between two dates. Since version 5.2, PHP has provided a DateTime class that can handle much more date and time information at the same time, rather than working with a plethora of separate date and time functions. Also, it works hand-in-hand with the new DateTimeZone class. We are looking at this class here in this chapter because it is a relatively new addition to PHP even though it is not strictly a new 5.3 feature set.

Timezone management has become more prominent in recent years with the onset of web portals and social web communities like Facebook and MySpace. Posting information to a website and having it recognize where you are in the world in relation to others on the same site is definitely a requirement these days. However, keep in mind that a function like date() will take the default information from the server on which the script is running, so unless the human client tells the server where she is in the world, it can be quite difficult to determine timezone location automatically.

There are a total of four interrelated classes that have to do with dates and times; we will look at three of them in this discussion. The constructor of the DateTime class is naturally where it all starts. This method takes two parameters: the timestamp and the timezone. Here is the syntax of a typical constructor method:

```
$dt = new DateTime("2010-02-12 16:42:33", new DateTimeZone('America/Halifax'));
```

This creates the $dt object and assigns it a date and time string with the first parameter and sets the timezone with the second parameter. The second parameter instantiates a new DateTimeZone object initially, then passes it through as the second parameter to the constructor. You can alternately instantiate the DateTimeZone object into its own variable and then use it in the DateTime constructor, like so:

```
$dtz = new DateTimeZone('America/Halifax') ;
$dt = new DateTime("2010-02-12 16:42:33", $dtz);
```

Obviously, we are assigning hardcoded values to these classes, and this type of information may not always be available to your code, or it may not be what you want. We can pick up the value of the timezone from the server's *.ini* file and use it inside the

`DateTimeZone` class. To pick up the current server value from the *.ini* file, use code similar to the following:

```
$timeZone = ini_get('date.timezone') ;
$dtz = new DateTimeZone($timeZone) ;
$dt = new DateTime("2010-02-12 16:42:33", $dtz);
```

Each of the code examples above merely establish a set of values for two classes, `DateTime` and `DateTimeZone`. Eventually, you will be using that information in some way elsewhere in your script. One of the methods of the `DateTime` class is called `format`, and it uses the same formatting output codes as the `date` function does. Those date format codes are all listed in Table 10-1. Here is a sample of the `format` method being sent to the browser as output:

```
echo "date: " . $dt->format("Y-m-d h:i:s");
```

The browser then shows the following output:

date: 2010-02-12 04:42:33

Table 10-1. Format characters for the DateTime class

Format character	Description
Day	
d	Day of the month, two digits with leading zeros [01 to 31]
D	A textual representation of a day, three letters [Mon through Sun]
j	Day of the month without leading zeros [1 to 31]
l (lowercase L)	A full textual representation of the day of the week [Sunday through Saturday]
N	ISO-8601 numeric representation of the day of the week (added in PHP 5.1.0) [1 (for Monday) through 7 (for Sunday)]
S	English ordinal suffix for the day of the month, two characters [st, nd, rd or th; works well with j]
Week	
w	Numeric representation of the day of the week [0 (for Sunday) through 6 (for Saturday)]
z	The day of the year (starting from 0) [0 through 365]
W	ISO-8601 week number of year, weeks starting on Monday (added in PHP 4.1.0) [Example: 42 (the 42nd week in the year)]
Month	
F	A full textual representation of a month, such as January or March [January through December]
m	Numeric representation of a month, with leading zeros [01 through 12]
M	A short textual representation of a month, three letters [Jan through Dec]
n	Numeric representation of a month, without leading zeros [1 through 12]
t	Number of days in the given month [28 through 31]

Year	
L	Whether it's a leap year [1 if it is a leap year, 0 otherwise]
o	ISO-8601 year number; this has the same value as Y, except that if the ISO week number (W) belongs to the previous or next year, that year is used instead (added in PHP 5.1.0) [Examples: 1999 or 2003]
Y	A full numeric representation of a year, four digits [Examples: 1999 or 2003]
y	A two-digit representation of a year [Examples: 99 or 03]

Time	
a	Lowercase Ante Meridiem and Post Meridiem [am or pm]
A	Uppercase Ante Meridiem and Post Meridiem [AM or PM]
B	Swatch Internet time [000 through 999]
g	12-hour format of an hour without leading zeros [1 through 12]
G	24-hour format of an hour without leading zeros [0 through 23]
h	12-hour format of an hour with leading zeros [01 through 12]
H	24-hour format of an hour with leading zeros [00 through 23]
i	Minutes with leading zeros [00 to 59]
s	Seconds with leading zeros [00 through 59]
u	Microseconds (added in PHP 5.2.2) [Example: 654321]

Timezone	
e	Timezone identifier (added in PHP 5.1.0) [Examples: UTC, GMT, Atlantic/Azores]
I (capital i)	Whether or not the date is in daylight savings time [1 if daylight savings time, 0 otherwise]
O	Difference from Greenwich mean time (GMT) in hours [Example: +0200]
P	Difference from GMT with colon between hours and minutes (added in PHP 5.1.3) [Example: +02:00]
T	Timezone abbreviation [Examples: EST, MDT]
Z	Timezone offset in seconds; the offset for timezones west of UTC is always negative, and for those east of UTC is always positive [-43200 through 50400]

Full date/time	
c	ISO-8601 date (added in PHP 5) [2004-02-12T15:19:21+00:00]
r	RFC 2822 formatted date [Example: Thu, 21 Dec 2000 16:01:07 +0200]
U	Seconds since the Unix Epoch (January 1 1970 00:00:00 GMT) [See also time()]

So far, we have provided the date and time to the constructor, but sometimes you will also want to pick up the date and time values from the server; to do this, simply provide the string "now" as the first parameter. The following code does the same as the other examples, except that it gets the date and time class values from the server; in fact, since it gets the information from the server, the class is much more fully populated:

```
$timeZone = ini_get('date.timezone') ;
$dtz = new DateTimeZone($timeZone) ;
$dt = new DateTime("now", $dtz);

echo "date: " . $dt->format("Y-m-d h:i:s");
```

The browser output shows the value from the server:

date: 2010-02-18 12:38:14

The `DateTime diff` method acts as you would expect; it returns the value of the difference between two dates. The catch here is that the result of the `diff` method is to instantiate and populate the `DateInterval` class. This class also has a `format` method, but because it deals with the difference between two dates, the format character codes are different. They are provided in Table 10-2.

Table 10-2. Format characters for the DateInterval class

Character description Each format character must be preceded by a percent (%) sign	Format
%	Literal %
Y	Years, numeric, at least two digits with leading 0 [01, 03]
y	Years, numeric [1, 3]
M	Months, numeric, at least 2 digits with leading 0 [01, 03, 12]
m	Months, numeric [1, 3, 12]
D	Days, numeric, at least 2 digits with leading 0 [01, 03, 31]
d	Days, numeric [1, 3, 31]
a	Total amount of days [4, 18, 8123]
H	Hours, numeric, at least 2 digits with leading 0 [01, 03, 23]
h	Hours, numeric [1, 3, 23]
I	Minutes, numeric, at least 2 digits with leading 0 [01, 03, 59]
i	Minutes, numeric [1, 3, 59]
S	Seconds, numeric, at least 2 digits with leading 0 [01, 03, 57]
s	Seconds, numeric [1, 3, 57]
R	Sign "−" when negative, "+" when positive [−, +]
r	Sign "−" when negative, empty when positive [−,]

So, to get the difference between two dates (two `DateTime` objects, more accurately), we write code like this:

```
$timeZone = ini_get('date.timezone') ;
$dtz = new DateTimeZone($timeZone) ;
```

```
$start_dt     = new DateTime("2009-02-12 16:42:33", $dtz);
$dt           = new DateTime("now", $dtz);

// creates a new instance of TimeInterval
$dt_diff      = $start_dt->diff($dt) ;

echo "<br/><br/>The difference between: " . $start_dt->format("Y-m-d")
. " and " . $dt->format("Y-m-d") . " is"
. $dt_diff->format('%y year, %m months, and %d days');
```

The diff method is called on one of the DateTime objects with the object of the other DateTime being passed in as a parameter. Then we prepare the browser output with the format method call.

Let's look a little more closely at the DateTimeZone class now. You can lift the timezone setting out of the *php.ini* file with the get_ini function that we have already seen. You can gather more information out of that timezone with the getLocation method. It provides the country of origin of the timezone, the longitude and the latitude, plus some comments. With these few lines of code, you have the beginnings of a web GPS system:

```
$timeZone = ini_get('date.timezone') ;
$dtz = new DateTimeZone($timeZone) ;

echo "Server's Time Zone: " . $timeZone . "<br/>";

foreach ( $dtz->getLocation() As $key => $value ){
    echo $key . " " . $value . "<br/>";
}
```

This produces the following browser output:

```
Server's Time Zone: America/Halifax
country_code CA
latitude 44.65
longitude −62.4
comments Atlantic Time - Nova Scotia (most places), PEI
```

If you want to set a timezone that is different from the server, pass that value to the constructor of the object. Here, we set the timezone for Rome, Italy, and display the information with the getLocation method. Notice that we pick up the set timezone with the getName method (even though we manually set it on the previous line of code):

```
$dtz = new DateTimeZone("Europe/Rome") ;

echo "Time Zone: " . $dtz->getName() . "<br/>";

foreach ( $dtz->getLocation() As $key => $value ){
    echo $key . " " . $value . "<br/>";
}
```

You can find a listing of available timezones at *http://www.php.net/man ual/en/timezones.php*.

There is a fair amount of date and time processing power provided in the classes that we have discussed and we have only covered the proverbial tip of the iceberg. Be sure to read more about these classes and what they can do on the PHP website (*http://php .net/index.php*).

Additional 5.3 Features

There are actually quite a lot of additional improvements to PHP with the release of version 5.3. Be sure to go to *http://www.php.net/ChangeLog-5.php* to check out the full listing of bug fixes and enhancements.

CHAPTER 11

Advanced Goodness

So far, this book has made an attempt to draw out the best of the PHP language. We have covered most of the basic concepts of PHP and discussed the cream of each topic. In this chapter, we'll look at some of the more advanced features of PHP and end with a summary of helpful references and resource materials so that you can go beyond this book into much deeper PHP waters if and when you so choose.

Regular Expressions

The first advanced area we will look at is that of regular expressions. Regular expressions provide a more advanced way to match patterns within a given string. Although there are many string functions available within PHP, there are still some tasks that you may want to perform that only a regular expression can accomplish. There are two types of regular expressions: Portable Operating System Interface for UniX (POSIX) and Perl-compatible. Because the Perl-compatible expressions are a little faster and more robust, we will only look at them here. There are three general uses for regular expressions: string matching, string substituting, and string splitting.

String Matching

Let's look at string matching first. When you are looking for a certain string or pattern within a provided string, you have to delimit the pattern. You generally do this with the forward slash character (/), but you can use any other nonalphanumeric character (other than the backslash) to do the same thing. So, if you are looking for a string pattern of "fox," you could set it up as /fox/ or #fox#, as long as you use the same characters on both ends of the pattern and they are not among the character pattern for which you are looking (e.g., if your pattern was fox#y, you would want to use /fox#y/ or {fox#y}, but not #fox#y#). The function to use for matching is preg_match: if a result is found, a 1 is returned (because it stops searching after the first occurrence found), and if nothing is found, a 0 is returned ("false" is returned if an error occurs). Consider the string: "the quick brown fox jumps over the lazy dog." We will use that to do some pattern matching. Here is the first sample:

```
$string = "The quick brown fox jumps over the lazy dog";
echo preg_match('/fox/', $string) ; // returns 1
```

Here we are looking for the string "fox" anywhere within the overall provided string. We could accomplish this with some of the more basic string functions that PHP provides, but the more complex part is still to come. The preg_match function also comes with some pattern quantifiers; Table 11-1 shows the most commonly used ones and examples of each.

Table 11-1. Pattern quantifiers for preg_match expressions

^	Test for the pattern at the beginning of the provided string.
$	Test for the pattern at the end of the provided string.
.	Match for any single character (wildcard).
\	General escape character, used when searching for other quantifiers as literal strings.
[]	Indicates that there is a possible range of valid characters: [0-5] means "between and including 0 and 5."
{}	Used to express how many characters are allowed within the previously defined pattern rule.

With these quantifiers, we can be much more specific in what we are looking for and where we are looking for it. Here are the promised examples:

```
echo preg_match('/^fox/', $string) ; // returns 0
echo preg_match('/^The/', $string) ; // returns 1
echo preg_match('/^the/', $string) ; // returns 0
echo preg_match('/dog$/', $string) ; // returns 1
echo preg_match('/f.x/', $string) ; // returns 1
```

Our final example is more complex: we will try to verify a North American phone number (with area code) in the pattern of 999-999-9999. We are looking for a first character in the range of 2 to 9 (North American area codes don't start with a 1); the next two characters in the range of 0 to 9; a hyphen followed by three digits, all in the range of 0 to 9; and another hyphen followed by four digits in the range of 0 to 9. It sounds complicated, and it is something that a basic string function just can't do efficiently (if at all). Here is the code that will accomplish this for us:

```
$phone_num = "903-543-5454";
$pattern = "/^[2-9]{1}[0-9]{2}-[0-9]{3}-[0-9]{4}$/" ;

echo preg_match($pattern, $phone_num) ; // returns true
```

Notice here that we can put our pattern into a variable as well so that it will lend itself to reuse. If, for example, we were testing home, fax, mobile, and work phone numbers, we can simply reuse the same pattern.

String Substituting

You can perform pattern searching and replacing with `preg_replace`, and the pattern definition rules remain the same. Here is an example using our "quick brown fox" string, replacing the word "fox" with "cheetah."

```
$string = "The quick brown fox jumps over the lazy dog" ;
echo preg_replace('/fox/', 'cheetah', $string) ;
```

The browser output is:

The quick brown cheetah jumps over the lazy dog

As a slightly more advanced example, let's look through that same phone number variable and change all instances of 4 to 7:

```
$phone_num = "903-543-5454";
echo preg_replace('/4/', '7', $phone_num) ;
```

Easy as this is, you may still want to replace a few different items at the same time to make things work a little faster. To accomplish this, simply send each search item as an array with a matching counterpoint in another array, like this:

```
$look_for = array("/4/", "/-/");
$replace_with = array('7', '*');
echo preg_replace($look_for, $replace_with, $phone_num) ;
```

Here we are attempting to replace all instances of 4 with 7 and all instances of – with *. The following output is produced:

903*573*5757

String Splitting

Another process that you can perform with regular expressions is extracting information from a string based on what is surrounding it. To do this, use the `preg_split` function. This takes a pattern you want to look for in a string, and the string itself, and returns the information that is not in the pattern. That may be a little confusing, so let's look at an example. Here we are looking for the operators in a math formula (our pattern), and we only want the digits (operands) returned. Preg_split returns what it locates as an array:

```
$pattern = "#[+*/-]#" ;
$formula = "36+15/5*12" ;
$operands = preg_split($pattern, $formula) ;
var_dump($operands) ;
```

The square brackets used here in the pattern tell the function to consider each item within them as single separate items to look for, and the use of the pound characters (#) is necessary, as our typical pattern delimiter (/) is actually one of the items we are looking for. The output is:

```
array(4) { [0]=> string(2) "36" [1]=> string(2) "15" [2]=> string(1) "5" [3]=> string(2)
"12" }
```

Regular expressions can be very powerful yet very complex. Tread in these waters carefully and, if you cannot accomplish what you want with the more simple PHP functions, by all means move on to explore these further. For further help and more complex examples, check out the page on the php.net site (*http://www.php.net/preg _match*).

SimpleXML

XML is gaining more and more strength in Web use each day. In its early days, it was just another way to share information between systems, but now it has become the frontrunner in the race for data sharing. PHP provides a few different ways to consume XML documents, and in this section we will look at the SimpleXML library (installed with PHP by default). It is meant for management of noncomplex XML documents, and you have to know the major elements of the target XML document in order to know what to expect and how to process its data accurately and properly. Consider the following well-formed XML document with three books defined within the library:

```xml
<?xml version="1.0" ?>
<library>
    <book>
        <title>Programming PHP, 2nd Ed.</title>
        <isbn>0-596-00681-0</isbn>
        <authors>
            <author>Rasmus Lerdorf</author>
            <author>Kevin Tatroe</author>
            <author>Peter MacIntyre</author>
        </authors>
        <publisher>OReilly</publisher>
        <price>39.99</price>
        <pubdate>April, 2006</pubdate>
    </book>
    <book>
        <title>PHP: The Good Parts</title>
        <isbn>978-0596804374</isbn>
        <authors>
            <author>Peter MacIntyre</author>
        </authors>
        <publisher>OReilly</publisher>
        <price>37.99</price>
        <pubdate>March, 2010</pubdate>
    </book>
    <book>
        <title>JavaScript: The Good Parts</title>
        <isbn>978-0-596-51774-8</isbn>
        <authors>
            <author>Douglas Crockford</author>
        </authors>
```

```
        <publisher>OReilly</publisher>
        <price>29.99</price>
        <pubdate>May, 2008</pubdate>
    </book>
</library>
```

This XML string will be saved into a variable named **$xml_data** and handed over to SimpleXML to process. Most times, you will collect a file from the hard drive or one provided to you by an outside source, but for our purposes here we will create the XML content ourselves. The only difference is in how you handle the XML file initially. SimpleXML is object-based, and therefore we can use the first line of the processing code (**$xml_doc = new SimpleXMLElement($xml_data);**) to hand the XML file to PHP as an object. The constructor of the class transforms the XML into multidimensional arrays (if the structure is that deep). We can then walk through the structure as if we were dealing with an array, employing the **foreach** construct to help us. As we walk through the levels of the XML file, we can then process the data as we see fit. In the following code, we echo the data out to the browser and test at one level to see if we have multiple authors for any book that should be listed together:

```php
$xml_doc = new SimpleXMLElement($xml_data);
foreach ($xml_doc as $book) {
    foreach ($book as $key=>$value) {
        if ($key == "authors") {
            echo $key . " = " ;
            foreach ($value as $author=>$detail) {
                echo $detail . ", ";
            }
        } else {
            echo $key . " = " . $value;
        }
        echo "<br/><br/>" ;
    }
}
```

This is basic XML processing; it's not very pretty, but you can do almost anything you want with this construct as you pass over the nodes of the XML structure. The above code produces the following raw output:

title = Programming PHP, 2nd Ed.

isbn = 0-596-00681-0

authors = Rasmus Lerdorf, Kevin Tatroe, Peter MacIntyre,

publisher = OReilly

price = 39.99

pubdate = April, 2006

title = PHP The Good Parts

isbn = 978-0596804374

authors = Peter MacIntyre,

publisher = OReilly

price = 37.99

pubdate = March, 2010

title = Javascript: The Good Parts

isbn = 978-0-596-51774-8

authors = Douglas Crockford,

publisher = OReilly

price = 29.99

pubdate = May, 2008

If you are reading a file in from a disk drive, you can use the following lines of code to test for its existence and then read it in for processing with the `simplexml_load_file` function. Both access methods create the same object construct for PHP to deal with, so you can use the previous **foreach** sample code:

```
if (file_exists('library.xml')) {
    $xml = simplexml_load_file('library.xml');
} else {
    // deal with the files non-existence
}
```

 There are two other SimpleXML functions that allow you to read data in for PHP processing, depending on the source of the XML data. `simplexml_load_string` is the functional equivalent of the code we used in the main example: `new SimpleXMLElement ($xml_data);`, which reads in a string of XML data for processing. The other one is `simplexml_import_dom`, which reads in XML from a Document Object Model (DOM) node.

Integrated Development Environments

Switching gears here, we should spend some time discussing a few of the best Integrated Development Environments (IDEs) that are out on the market for PHP development.

There are a number of good ones out there, though many are merely advanced text editors, so we won't be discussing those. The front runners are Komodo, Zend Studio for Eclipse, and PhpED. Each has specific strengths, so be sure to evaluate each one based on what you want to do within your development efforts. Following is a brief description of the major features of each.

 This is not meant to endorse any particular product or to exclude any other great IDEs on the market. We are merely giving you a taste for what is out there.

Komodo by ActiveState

The Komodo IDE by ActiveState (*http://www.activestate.com/komodo/*) is a multilanguage environment, which means that you can use it to develop in PHP, Python, Ruby, ASP, JavaScript, and so on. This is one of its strongest selling points. It therefore lends itself to use by programmers who are responsible for maintaining a lot of disparate web environments. Here is how ActiveState currently describes its product:

> Whatever Your Language: Komodo IDE supports PHP, Python, Ruby, Perl and Tcl, plus JavaScript, CSS, HTML and template languages like RHTML, Template-Toolkit, HTML-Smarty and Django.

> Whatever Your Platform: Mac? Linux? Windows? Yes, yes, and yes! Buy just one license and use it on all your platforms.

> Work Smarter, Not Harder: Komodo IDE's award-winning feature set includes standard editor functionality, syntax checking and coloring, a regex debugging tool, and more. And it's extensible, so hack away.

> Share the Workload: Team development is faster with source code control integration, a project manager and multi-user support.

Zend Studio for Eclipse

Zend Studio for Eclipse (*http://www.zend.com/en/products/studio/*) is a very strong and robust IDE. It is very well integrated with many of the other tools that Zend has to offer, which is a great advantage if you are thinking of becoming a *Zend Shop*. Since it is based on the Eclipse platform, Studio is also able to use any of the many add-on products that are part of the Eclipse environment, not just other Zend products. Team development through either SubVersion (SVN) or Concurrent Versions System (CVS) integration, code highlighting, syntax checking, robust debugging, code profiling, and task management are just a few of its many features. Here is what Zend says about its own product:

> Zend Studio 7.0 is the next generation of our professional-grade PHP application development environment. It has been designed to maximize developer productivity by

enabling you to develop and maintain code faster, solve application problems quickly, and improve team collaboration.

Zend Studio is the only IDE designed for professional developers that encompasses all the development components necessary for the full PHP application lifecycle. Through a comprehensive set of editing, debugging, analysis, optimization, database tools, and testing, Zend Studio speeds development cycles and simplifies complex projects.

PhpED by NuSphere

PhpED (*http://www.nusphere.com/*) is a good editor for small- to mid-sized projects. There are three versions, with additional features available for the higher prices. Although it is only available for the Windows platform, it is still a very versatile editor with a built-in code highlighter and code folder. Additionally, it is project-based, so you can manage different projects at the same time (in each coding session). PhpED supports team development with CVS integration, but does not support SVN code management. This is what NuSphere says about it on its home page:

> PhpED is the PHP IDE helping PHP developers take advantage of the latest cutting technology. PhpED version 5.9 brings you the full support of PHP 5.3 features, including namespaces, objects import, closures, class level constants (keyword const) now-doc and more. PhpED 5.9 comes on the tail of version 5.8, which was dedicated to the Web 2.0 stack of development tools in our PHP IDE. Your PHP IDE support for PHP 5.3 features is provided at every level through out PhpED, starting from dynamic syntax highlighting to parsers, code completion, and PHP debugger. PhpED IDE support for previous versions of PHP is also enhanced.

Primary Websites

As a further point of reference, I want to share with you the primary websites that I visit on a regular basis. You will find them to be a great resource for your development, your problem solving, and your code debugging. There are countless PHP websites out there, to be sure, but I hope to save you some Google time by including the references within these pages.

php.net

http://www.php.net is the home of the PHP language where the releases of the language files and maintenance of the reference library (with syntax use explanations and examples) are kept. One neat feature of this site is that it allows for the addition of user comments. This allows the developer community to contribute best practices, lessons learned, and "gotchas" on a function-by-function basis. It also contains information about upcoming user group meetings on a monthly basis. If you can locate a PHP user group close to where you live or work, you should try to attend some of its functions; it's a great way to get to know other PHP developers in your area and to see what is being done with PHP close to home. Figure 11-1 shows a screen shot of the php.net home page at the time of this writing.

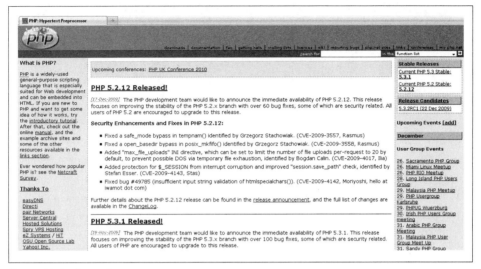

Figure 11-1. php.net home page

zend.com

http://www.zend.com is the home page of Zend Corporation. This is more of the commercial side of PHP, where "the PHP Company" has many products for sale (including Studio, discussed earlier) as well as training courses and support services. Here, you can also find out all the latest Zend news and developments as PHP gains more and more ground in the web development world. You can order Zend Certification training and tests here, and you can search through the PHP Yellow Pages for programmers who have passed the Zend PHP exam. Figure 11-2 shows the zend.com home page at the time of this writing.

devzone.zend.com

Another great resource is the DevZone website (*http://www.devzone.zend.com*) run by Zend. It's a support and best practice area for all Zend products. Although the website subtitle is, "Advancing the art of PHP," it has resources (articles, tutorials, podcasts, book reviews, webinars, and forums) for all Zend product lines. This is a wonderful place to seek out articles or white papers on almost any PHP-related topic, and the PHP online manual is here as well. Figure 11-3 shows what the Zend DevZone home page looks like at the time of this writing.

Figure 11-2. zend.com home page

Figure 11-3. devzone.zend.com home page

phparch.com

The last must-have bookmark is the *php|architect* website (*http://www.phparch.com*). This is primarily a website for promotion of the *php|architect* magazine, which is available in traditional paper format as well as PDF format. This is a super technical magazine that has been in publication for several years now. Full disclosure: I am a past editor for the magazine, so I may be biased, but I can also speak to its high quality and excellent content. Apart from publishing the magazine, the organization that runs it also usually hosts two PHP conferences per calendar year. These conferences are great to attend and a good way to meet lots of people in the PHP community. Getting back to the website, though, you will find some excellent books, podcasts, and training materials. There is also an online news thread that allows you to keep up on all the late-breaking news in the PHP world. Figure 11-4 shows what the phparch.com home page looks like at the time of this writing.

Figure 11-4. phparch.com home page

PHP/Web Conferences

A number of great PHP and web conferences are hosted each year all over the world. In addition to the ones already mentioned (hosted by the *php|architect* folks), there is a major one held each fall in California and hosted by Zend Corporation, known as ZendCon. There are also many conferences held in Europe (England, Spain, and Germany), South America (Rio), and Canada (PHP Quebec) that are worth looking into. The best way to locate these conferences is to check out the conference listings page (*http://www.php.net/conferences*). Here you will be able to see when conferences are and if there is an open call for proposals. Feel free to submit a topic proposal; it's always great to hear new and interesting ideas from a broad range of speakers.

There are a vast number of other PHP resources out on the Web, in blogs, and in book form. Take some time to look through some of the links that are offered on the websites mentioned above and use your preferred search engine to help you find even more resources. And in the true nature of the open source philosophy, be sure to share any gold nuggets that you find.

The Bad Parts

PHP having bad parts is difficult to comprehend. After all, it is one of the most widely used software development languages in the world. NASA, Wikipedia, Yahoo!, and IBM, among others, all use it day in and day out for their critical data processing and web development. In fact, it has been my opinion that PHP does not have any really bad parts, just some potentially tricky areas to be aware of and work around.

However, after some deep soul searching, I came to realize that PHP is not perfect—how could it be? It was created by humans (imperfect beings) and newer versions are being produced all the time (with bug fixes included). Having said that, we will spend the few remaining pages looking at the weaknesses (or perceived weaknesses) of PHP, as well as ways to either work around them or avoid them altogether.

goto

The first item to discuss here is the inclusion of a goto statement in PHP version 5.3. This is one of those items that, in my opinion, should only be used by those with enough experience to not get themselves trapped in an infinite loop. As you may recall from Chapter 10, there are a number of potential coding follies that you can get yourself into. Nothing truly safeguards you against writing code similar to that shown in the following listing:

```
landing15:
goto landing15;
```

 Actually, PHP has an *.ini* setting directive that will stop a script that runs too long with a default setting of 30 seconds—it's called max_execution_time. If the time limit is exceeded, the guilty script is terminated, so you won't be able to cripple your server (but infinite loops are certainly still something to try to avoid).

This is indeed a potentially bad part of PHP, but only if you are inept enough to actually write something like this. This is not really the fault of PHP. Again, we are looking at an area of code writing that is at the mercy of the skill and logic of the programmer. PHP gives you all kinds of rope, and it's up to you as the developer not to hang yourself (or others).

Function Naming and Parameter Order

As you may remember, PHP is an open source product. This means that it is written and developed by many programmers all over the world. So it follows that there are many cultures and spoken languages influencing the project. Mass confusion could result, but there are balances and controls in place for the most part, and Zend is helping to keep an eye on things. Still, there are many instances in the PHP language where naming conventions are not followed consistently. For example, you will see some internal functions named with an underscore, like `var_dump` or `strip_tags`, while others will be continuous, like `stripslashes` and `strpos`. This can be a great annoyance for sure, since you will undoubtedly be forced to look up function names to verify their exact syntax, and not just a few times.

There is another level of inconsistency that can also trip you up: the position of the parameters in string functions is the reverse of the parameters in array functions when you are searching for content. If you look on the *php.net* website (*http://php.net/index .php*), you will see that the online documentation refers to these parameters as `$needle` and `$haystack`. As an example, the syntax for the `strstr` function is this:

```
strstr ( string $haystack , mixed $needle [, bool $before_needle = false ] )
```

And the syntax for the `array_search` function looks like this:

```
array_search ( mixed $needle , array $haystack [, bool $strict ] )
```

It is a bit of a hassle to try to keep this kind of information straight. Obviously, these subsystems in PHP were written by different developers, or by one developer who forgot what he was doing (also notice that one uses an underscore for the function name and one does not—more potential confusion).

So the only real way to keep this all in order is to memorize the fact that array functions want the needle parameter first and string functions want the haystack information first, and one or both may or may not use an underscore.

 This is one aspect of PHP that makes getting certified all that much more valuable. If you can pass the certification exam and keep this kind of information straight, you should be a good candidate for a high-paying development job!

Loose Typing

The next area that we will look at as a possible weakness of PHP is in the area of variable data type declaration. PHP is *loosely typed*, which means you do not have to declare the kind or type of data (integer, string, float, etc.) that will be stored in a variable. PHP does its best to figure that out on its own. The alternative to this is called *strong typing*, in which a variable is "told" what kind of data it will hold at the moment of its creation. For PHP code, you could use a variable called $notes and assign a string of text to it and, on the very next line, store integer data into it. Although this may inject bugs into your logic, PHP would be unaffected in how it processed the code.

Herein lies the issue: once a variable is "typed," PHP can reassign its value, if so directed. This can lead to confusion on the part of the developer, since the code has the potential to change content. This can make code debugging and maintenance very difficult.

Some would argue the opposite, however, and say that this is an elegant way to manage variables—let the code engine do the work and just let the developer create her masterpiece (even if it may be difficult to maintain later). So, again, this is not necessarily a bad part of PHP, but rather something to be aware of and adapt to when the need arises.

Register Globals

The last topic to be discussed as a bad part is really only so because of a potential security breach in its use. You can turn the register_globals directive on or off in the *php.ini* file. In recent versions (4.2.0 and later), it is turned off by default. You can also manage this setting within a running PHP script with the ini_set function.

register_globals is actually quite a timesaver and if it weren't for the security hole, I think it would be used much more widely. It creates variables in memory based on a submitted HTML form. So, if you have a data entry form that asks for lastname and firstname when the form is submitted (with register_globals turned on), variables called $lastname and $firstname are automatically created for you on the subsequently called page, with any entered data loaded into them for you.

The security flaw is that the PHP script is then open to data injection. If, for example, a form is submitted with the GET action and it has an input with the name lname for last name, someone can inject a value into that field through the URL address. This injection can be bad data, malicious JavaScript code, or even some unwanted SQL commands.

If you are using a version of PHP prior to 4.2.0, make sure you either turn off this directive (if you have the power to do so at the server level) or turn it off with the ini_set function. If you can't turn it off, be sure to avoid its use.

`register_globals` is a deprecated directive and it will disappear from PHP in the next full version release (version 6.0). The only reason it is still available is for backward compatibility.

Is That All?

There may be other areas of PHP that people in the development community consider to be "bad," though, as I have stated earlier, it is really a matter of perspective and experience. PHP is growing in strength, popularity, and use, and can only get better and better over time.

Keep in mind that PHP is an open source programming language and that its improvements are created by contributions from the user community. If you are interested in getting involved with making PHP "bad part free," be sure to get involved at *http://www.php.net*.

Index

Symbols

& for referenced variables, 10, 30
<?php text sequence, 4
\ (backslash)
    for escaping characters, 34
    for namespace identification, 122
    removing escapes from output, 113–115
    stripping from strings, 41
[ ]
    for referencing arrays, 46, 48
    in regular expressions, 135
{ }
    for code blocks, 27
    for defining namespaces, 120
$ for variable names, 9
$_ prefix for superglobals, 21
( ) for functions, 27
| | (OR) condition test, 16
++ command, 19
# for inline comments, 8
' (single quotes) for strings, 34
    in array keys, 47
" (double quotes) for strings, 34
    in array keys, 47
/* ... */ for multiline comments, 8
// for inline comments, 8

A

a+ option (file management functions), 84
accessor methods, 69–70
ActiveState Komodo IDE, 139
Add method (PieGraph class), 105
adding elements to arrays, 48
AddLink method (FPDF), 99

addresses of SMS domains, 91
addslashes function, 41, 115
AliasNbPages method (FPDF), 97
anonymous functions (closures), 122
antispam graphics, generating, 109
array function, 46
array functions, 51–57, 146
    math-type functions, 53
    sorting array elements, 51–53
        randomly, 54
array_merge function, 56
array_rand function, 54
array_search function, 54
array_splice function, 49
array_sum function, 54
array_unique function, 54
array_walk function, 57
arrays, 45–57
    associative arrays, 46
    for data validation, 112
    dynamic, 48–50
    indexed arrays, 45
    multidimensional, 47
    reading files into, 86
    traversing, 50, 57
arsort function, 51
asort function, 51
assigning values to function parameters, 30
assigning values to variables, 10
assignment expression, 13
associative arrays, 46
    merging, 56
AUTO_INCREMENT option (SQLite), 78
averaging array values, 54

B

backslash (\)
    for escaping characters, 34
    for namespace identification, 122
    removing escapes from output, 113–115
    stripping from strings, 41
bar charts, generating, 107–108
break statements, 17
browser tabs, 22
BuildTable method (FPDF), 102–104
built-in functions, 32
by-reference assignment, 10, 30
by-value assignment, 10, 30

C

callback functions, unnamed, 123
calling functions, 27
capitalization of strings, functions for, 38
captchas, generating, 109
case management (strings), 38
cell, document (FPDF), 93
cell method (FPDF), 93, 104
character case management, 38
characters, escaping, 34
    removing escapes from output, 113–115
    stripping backslashes from strings, 41
classes, 59
    creating objects from, 65
    inheritance, 60
    namespaces, 119–122
closures (anonymous functions), 122
comment lines, 8
community server, 71
compact function, 55
compound data types, 10, 45
concatenating arrays, 56
condition testing (see flow control)
conditional return statements, 28
constants, 11–13
__construct method, 65
constructor methods, 65
$_COOKIE superglobal, 21, 111
cookies, 20, 111
count function, 54
counting array elements, 54
cross-site scripting (XXS), 115–116

D

data encryption, 116–117
data management using files, 79–87
data types, 9
    of array elements, 47
    loose typing, 147
    in SQLite, 78
data validation, 111–113
    in set methods, 70
database interaction, 71–87
    escaping data for, 114
    file management as alternative to, 79–87
    MySQLi object interface, 71–74
    PHP Data Objects (PDO), 74–77
    SQLite database tool, 77–79
date and time functions, 126–131
DateInterval class, 129
DateTime class, 126–131
DateTimeZone class, 126–131
day format (DateTime), 127, 129
decision-making constructs (see flow control)
default DateTime information, 126
default function parameters, 29, 68
define function, 11
defined constants, 11–13
defining functions, 27
deleting elements from arrays, 49
__destruct method, 66
destructor methods, 66
development environments
    PHP, 138–140
    setting up, 3
DevZone website, 141
diff method (DateTime), 129
difference between dates, 129
directories, creating, 82
do...while... construct, 18
document cell (FPDF), 93
documents, PDF (see FPDF library)
documents, XML (see SimpleXML library)
domains, SMS, 91
double quotes (") for strings, 34
    in array keys, 47
dynamic arrays, 48–50
dynamic PDFs, 102–104

E

echo command, 4, 34

H

headers, PDF documents, 96
Hello World program, 4
HEREDOC constructs, 35, 123
histograms, generating, 107–108
history of PHP, 1
hour format (DateTime), 129
html class (example), 60
HTML entities, 41
html_entity_decode function, 41
HTML tags, stripping from strings, 40
htmlentities function, 41, 114
htmlspecialchars function, 113
HTTP GET method, 23, 24
HTTP POST method, 23, 24
hyperlinks in PDF documents, 97–100

I

IDEs for PHP programming, 138–140
if statements, 14–16
Image method (FPDF), 98
images in PDF documents, 97–100
in_array function, 54
includable files, 65
include_once statement, 32
include statement, 31–32
indexed arrays, 45
    merging, 56
inheritance, 60
.ini file (see php.ini settings file)
ini_set function, 147
injection attacks, 115–116, 147
inline comments, 8
input data validation, 111–113
    in set methods, 70
installing PHP, 3
installing PHPMailer library, 90
instantiation, 65
integrated development environments, 138–140
integration with web pages, 19–25
    cookies, 20, 111
    $_GET superglobal, 22, 111
    $_POST superglobal, 23, 111
    $_REQUEST superglobal, 24
    sessions, 21, 111
internal links, PDF documents, 99

interpolative characteristics of double quotes, 34, 35
is_int function, 113
is_numeric function, 113
is_readable function, 86
is_writable function, 86

J

JPGraph library, 105–109
jumping within code files (see goto statement)

K

key/value pairs, 45
keys, array
    naming, 46
    numerical (indexed arrays), 45
    selecting randomly, 54
    strings for, 46
Komodo IDE (ActiveState), 139
krsort function, 51
ksort function, 51

L

latitude information, 130
layout options, PDF files, 96
lcfirst function, 38
length of strings, returning, 39
Lerdorf, Rasmus, 1
libraries, PHP
    FPDF library, 92–104
    JPGraph library, 105–109
    PHPMailer library, 89–92
    SimpleXML library, 136–138
links in PDF documents, 97–100
locking files, 84
longitude information, 130
looping, endless, 125
loose typing, 147
lowercase in strings, functions for, 38
ltrim function, 36

M

magic methods, 65
mail function, 89–92
matching strings with regular expressions, 133–134
math-type array functions, 53

PHPMailer library, 89–92
phpmailer.php file, 90
pie charts, generating, 105–107
polymorphism, 59
POST method (HTTP), 23, 24
$_POST superglobal, 23, 111
precedence, included or required files, 32
preg_match function, 133
preg_replace function, 135
preg_split function, 135
prepared statements (PDO), 75
primitive types, 10
print command, 34
private scope, 68
programming resources, 140
properties, 59
    get and set methods, 69–70
    scope of, 68
protected scope, 68
public scope, 68

Q

queryexec method, 79
quote function, 115
quotes for strings, 34
    in array keys, 47

R

random extraction of array value, 54
random sorting of array values, 54
randomizing string content, 42
real_escape_string function, 115
receiving parameters (see default function
        parameters)
reference approach to parameter assignment,
        30
reference approach to variable assignment, 10
references, websites on PHP, 140
referencing array elements, 46, 47
    traversing array elements, 50, 57
register_globals directive, 118, 147
regular expressions, 133–136
    splitting strings, 135
    string matching, 133–134
    substituting strings, 135
removing elements from arrays, 49
replacing strings, 40
reports, graphical, 105–109

$_REQUEST superglobal, 24
require_once statement, 32
require statement, 31–32
resources for further reading, 140
retrieving database data for display, 73
return values (see functions)
rsort function, 51
rtrim function, 36

S

salt-and-pepper encryption, 117
scalar data types, 10, 45
scope
    defined constants, 11
    of properties, 68
    variables, 11
scripting attacks, 115–116
searching arrays, 54
searching strings, 39–40
second format (DateTime), 129
security, 111–118
    cross-site scripting and SQL injection, 115–
        116
    input data validation, 70, 111–113
    output validation, 113–115
    password encryption, 116–117
    register_globals directive, 118, 147
server value for timezone, 126
session.save_path directive, 22
session_start function, 22
$_SESSION superglobal, 22, 111
sessions, 21, 111
set methods, 69–70
setcookie function, 21
SetLink method (FPDF), 99
SetX method (FPDF), 94, 101
SetY method (FPDF), 101
sha1 encryption algorithm, 116
shuffle function, 54
SimpleXML library, 136–138
simplexml_import_dom function, 138
simplexml_load_file function, 138
simplexml_load_string function, 138
single quotes (') for strings, 34
    in array keys, 47
size of file, determining, 84
size of strings, returning, 39
SMS generation, 89–92
sort function, 51

About the Author

Peter B. MacIntyre has over 20 years of experience in the information technology industry, primarily in the area of software development. His technical skillset includes several web development languages, client/server tools, and relational database systems, including PHP, MySQL, PowerBuilder, Visual Basic, Active Server Pages, and CA-Visual Objects. He is a Zend Certified Engineer, having passed his PHP 4.x Certification Exam, and he is very proud to have been the first person in Atlantic Canada to earn that designation.

Over the years, Peter has developed several large-scale systems using PowerBuilder with Sybase SQL Anywhere, as well as several X-base systems in the Clipper programming language for the government of Prince Edward Island. He also has considerable expertise in data modeling/architecture, including both logical and physical database design.

Peter has contributed content to four IT industry publications: *Using Visual Objects* (Que Corporation), *Using PowerBuilder 5* (Que Corporation), *ASP.NET Bible* (Wiley Press), and *The Web Warrior Guide to Web Programming* (Thompson Course Technology), and has provided technical editing services for eight additional books. Peter is a coauthor of *Programming PHP*, Second Edition (*http://oreilly.com/catalog/9780596006815/*) (O'Reilly), which has been translated into three European languages, and *Zend Studio for Eclipse Developer's Guide* (Addison-Wesley). He was formerly a contributing editor and author for the magazine *php|architect* (*www.phparch.com*).

Peter has spoken at North American and international computer conferences, including CA-World in New Orleans, USA; CA-TechniCon in Cologne, Germany; and CA-Expo in Melbourne, Australia.

Peter lives and works in Prince Edward Island, Canada, where he is a program manager (chief systems architect) for MJL Enterprises (*www.mjlfirst.com*), a company that specializes in web and mobile web applications for the automotive and insurance industries. He also runs his own part-time software company called Paladin Business Solutions (*www.paladin-bs.com*), and he can be contacted through its website.

Colophon

The animal on the cover of *PHP: The Good Parts* is a Booted Racket-tail hummingbird (*Ocreatus underwoodii*). The Booted Racket-tail is a species that, as its name suggests, is noted for a pair of distinctive features: a split tail that is sometimes thought to resemble a pair of tennis rackets with elongated handles and small heads, and legs clad with downy white feathers, causing the bird to appear to be wearing boots. Female Booted Racket-tails also sport white breast plumage.

The Booted Racket-tail is a South American variety of hummingbird, and can be found along the Andean cordillera, in the rainforests of Bolivia, Ecuador, Peru, and Venezuela. Because of its fairly widespread habitat, the bird is considered relatively common in western South America. Nonetheless, Booted Racket-tails are a popular subject for birdwatchers and photographers visiting the region, likely due to the species' distinctive appearance.

In 2004, researchers from the University of California, Berkeley, and the California Institute of Technology included Booted Racket-tails in a study of Peruvian hummingbirds intended to discover why the species remained mostly at lower altitudes, as opposed to venturing up higher where there is less competition for food. Not surprisingly, the researchers noted that at higher altitudes, where the air is thinner, the hummingbirds demonstrated a loss of power and maneuverability, hampering their ability to thrive.

An image of Booted Racket-tails also appeared on a 1996 Ecuadorian postage stamp.

The cover image is from *Cassell's Natural History*. The cover font is Adobe ITC Garamond. The text font is Linotype Birka; the heading font is Adobe Myriad Condensed; and the code font is LucasFont's TheSansMonoCondensed.

Get even more for your money.

Join the O'Reilly Community, and register the O'Reilly books you own.It's free, and you'll get:

- 40% upgrade offer on O'Reilly books
- Membership discounts on books and events
- Free lifetime updates to electronic formats of books
- Multiple ebook formats, DRM FREE
- Participation in the O'Reilly community
- Newsletters
- Account management
- 100% Satisfaction Guarantee

Signing up is easy:

1. **Go to: oreilly.com/go/register**
2. **Create an O'Reilly login.**
3. **Provide your address.**
4. **Register your books.**

Note: English-language books only

To order books online:

oreilly.com/order_new

For questions about products or an order:

orders@oreilly.com

To sign up to get topic-specific email announcements and/or news about upcoming books, conferences, special offers, and new technologies:

elists@oreilly.com

For technical questions about book content:

booktech@oreilly.com

To submit new book proposals to our editors:

proposals@oreilly.com

Many O'Reilly books are available in PDF and several ebook formats. For more information:

oreilly.com/ebooks

O'REILLY®

Spreading the knowledge of innovators   www.oreilly.com

Buy this book and get access to the online edition for 45 days—for free!

PHP: The Good Parts

By Peter MacIntyre
April 2010, $29.99
ISBN 9780596804374

With Safari Books Online, you can:

Access the contents of thousands of technology and business books

- Quickly search over 7000 books and certification guides
- Download whole books or chapters in PDF format, at no extra cost, to print or read on the go
- Copy and paste code
- Save up to 35% on O'Reilly print books
- **New!** Access mobile-friendly books directly from cell phones and mobile devices

Stay up-to-date on emerging topics before the books are published

- Get on-demand access to evolving manuscripts.
- Interact directly with authors of upcoming books

Explore thousands of hours of video on technology and design topics

- Learn from expert video tutorials
- Watch and replay recorded conference sessions

To try out Safari and the online edition of this book FREE for 45 days, go to **www.oreilly.com/go/safarienabled** and enter the coupon code SPQPFDB. To see the complete Safari Library, visit safari.oreilly.com.

Spreading the knowledge of innovators   safari.oreilly.com